Robert Owen and the architect Joseph Hansom

An unlikely form of co-operation

For Harry and Emily

Robert Owen and the architect Joseph Hansom

An unlikely form of co-operation

Penelope Harris

BREWIN BOOKS

BREWIN BOOKS
19 Enfield Ind. Estate,
Redditch,
Worcestershire,
B97 6BY
www.brewinbooks.com

Published by Brewin Books 2020

© Penelope Harris, 2020

The author has asserted her rights in accordance with the Copyright, Designs and Patents Act 1988 to be identified as the author of this work.

All rights reserved. No part of this publication may be reproduced, stored in a retrieval system, or transmitted in any form or by any means, electronic, mechanical, photocopying, recording or otherwise, without the prior permission in writing of the publisher and the copyright owners, or as expressly permitted by law, or under terms agreed with the appropriate reprographics rights organization. Enquiries concerning reproduction outside the terms stated here should be sent to the publishers at the UK address printed on this page.

The publisher makes no representation, express or implied, with regard to the accuracy of the information contained in this book and cannot accept any legal responsibility for any errors or omissions that may be made.
A CIP catalogue record for this book is available from the British Library.

ISBN: 978-1-85858-717-2

Printed and bound in Great Britain
by Severn.

CONTENTS

LIST OF ILLUSTRATIONS 7
ABBREVIATIONS 9
INTRODUCTION 10

I   ROBERT OWEN – a man with a vision 17
     Early years 17
     New Lanark 20
     New Harmony 30

II   JOSEPH HANSOM – an architect with a social conscience . . 43
     Early years 43
     Birmingham 46
     Hinckley 56

III   BIRMINGHAM – the town, the people and politics 70
     Early years 70
     Attwood, Pare, McDonnell, O'Connell and Ireland 75
     Birmingham Political Union, Labour notes, Equitable Labour Exchanges, General National Consolidated Trades Union . . 80

IV   NEW BEGINNINGS – Owen's millennium 92
     Early communities 92
     From Queen Wood Farm to Harmony Hall 96
     From Harmony Hall to Queenwood College 98

V	THE AFTERMATH – where next?	116
	Owen	116
	Hansom	119
	Epilogue	122

APPENDICES		131
I	Time line	131
II	Short biographies	134

SELECT BIBLIOGRAPHY	146
INDEX	151

LIST OF ILLUSTRATIONS

	Robert Owen and Joseph Hansom	Front cover
	Birmingham Town Hall – artist's impression by W. Harris, 1831	Front cover
	Harmony Hall (later Queenwood College) showing avenue of yews – kind permission Hampshire Record Office, 6M7/G3	Front cover
1.	Old Newtown – kind permission RO Museum	36
2.	Robert Owen memorial, Newtown – author's photograph	37
3.	Old New Lanark – kind permission RO Museum	38
4.	New Lanark School House – author's photograph	39
5.	Dancing class by G. Hunt – kind permission New Lanark Trust	40
6.	Owen's Plan	41
7.	The Crisis 1832	42
8.	Engraving of York 1840 by W. Harvey – kind permission York Museum Trust (York Art Gallery), YORAG-R43	61
9.	Beaumaris – author's photographs:	
	(a) Beaumaris gaol	62
	(b) Bulkeley Arms Hotel	62
	(c) Victoria Terrace	62
	(d) Trainer's (Chantry) House	62
10.	Attwood and Spooner bank – kind permission Birmingham Museum and Art Galley Picture Library, 1932V264/23	63
11.	Raising Rafters – *Architectural Magazine*, vol.2, 1835	64
12.	Memorial of Badger and Heap – Wiki commons	65
13.	Notice of Builders' Union – kind permission Co-operative College	66
14.	Operative Builders' Guildhall – *The Pioneer*, 23 December 1833, p.137	67
15.	Banner regarding Derby Lockout – photograph Bill Whitehead	68
16.	Notification of Builders' College – *The Builder,* precursor, 31 December 1842, p.6	69
17.	Engraving of Birmingham from the South, drawn by W. Harvey, showing Town Hall on horizon – kind permission of Birmingham Museum and Art Gallery Picture Library, 1996V146/5	87
18.	Thomas Attwood reclining on steps outside Town Hall – author's photograph	88
19.	Newhall Hill Meeting – Dent, *Making of Birmingham*, vol.2, p.360	89

20.	Bromsgrove Lickey Memorial – author's photograph	90
21.	(a) Rational Medals – Dent, *Old and New Birmingham*, vol.2, p.419	91
	(b) National Equitable Labour Exchange Note	91
22.	South London Rational School, 3 Blackfriars Road – McCabe, *Robert Owen*, p.75	110
23.	Location of the community in the parish of East Tytherley – kind permission Edward Royle	111
24.	Comparison of Hansom's H-plans:	
	(a) Plan of one pair floor, Harmony Hall – Senate House Special Collection, William Pare Scrapbook, M.S. 578, 1839	112
	(b) Training College for Catholic Schoolmistresses, Hansom 1857 – kind permission Nuns of Notre Dame de Namur	112
25.	Harmony Hall (later Queenwood College) showing avenue of yews – kind permission Hampshire Record Office, 6M7/G3	113
26.	Tulketh Hall – u.d., private collection	114
27.	Extant kitchen wall at Tytherley – courtesy Hampshire Garden Trust	115
28.	(a) Gravestone of Robert Owen – author's photograph	125
	(b) Gravestone of Joseph Hansom – photograph Hazel Evinson	125
29.	Remains of St Mary's Church, Leeds – photograph James Hughes	126
30.	(a) St Walburge's Church, Preston – photograph Peter Ellis	127
	(b) St Mary and St Boniface Cathedral church, Plymouth – author's photograph	127
31.	(a) St Beuno's College, showing terracing – kind permission St Beuno's Jesuit Spirituality Centre	128
	(b) St Beuno's College, showing greenhouse – permission as above	128
32.	Todmorden Town Hall – photograph Andy Caveney	129
33.	Hansom cab rank in Colmore Row – u.d., source unknown	130
34.	William Allen – *Millgate*, vol.24, 1928	134
35.	Thomas Attwood – portrait by W. Green, Birmingham Museum and Art Gallery, 1978P253	135
36.	George Holyoake – kind permission RO Museum	139
37.	William Maclure – kind permission, The Academy of Natural Sciences of Philadelphia, Drexel University	140
38.	Thomas McDonnell – kind permission Clifton Diocese Archives	140
39.	Daniel O'Connell – public domain	142
40.	William Pare – source unknown	142
41.	Johann Pestalozzi – public domain	144

ABBREVIATIONS

AA	*Anglesey Archives*
BJ	*Birmingham Journal*
BPU	Birmingham Political Union
BTH	Birmingham Town Hall
GNCTU	Grand National Consolidated Trades Union
HH	Harmony Hall
NMW	*New Moral World*
ODNB	*Oxford Dictionary of National Biographies*
RIBA	Royal Institute of British Architects
UCL	University College London

INTRODUCTION

When compiling his autobiography in 1857, Owen said 'The mission of my life appears to be, to prepare the population of the world to understand the vast importance of the second creation of humanity' and 'to point out to humanity the way to remove from it the cause of sin and misery ... and attain for all of our race a new existence of universal goodness, wisdom, and happiness ... which appear to arise from new surroundings'.[1] Joseph Hansom said 'All we require is to turn the talent with which heaven is blessed to us to the best account'.[2] Two very different statements from two very different people who, nevertheless, had much in common. Certainly the combination of Robert Owen, an atheist visionary and social reformer, and Joseph Hansom, a budding Roman Catholic architect, is at first glance an unlikely one.

When researching for a preliminary biography of Hansom, two seemingly inexplicable phrases from work carried out by others jumped off the pages. The one was reference to the influence of the French Revolution and the other described Hansom as 'the Socialist Architect'.[3] These needed further investigation. Initially unaware of the seismic effect the rapidly changing social conditions had upon shaping both their lives and how it brought them together, this element, along with the realisation of how much disturbances in France had impacted on England, underpinned the reasoning behind this book. It centres on the period between 1829 (Owen's return from America), and 1845 (the demise of his third and final social community). 1834 was the most critical year in terms of life-changing events. The aim is not to replicate previous biographies (in which case it would be sadly deficient due to its many omissions), but to focus specifically on the political, social, economic and religious upheavals which took both men to Birmingham and ultimately to a remote part of Hampshire. Birmingham, and its first MP Thomas Attwood, was the driving force behind the Great Reform Bill of 1832, the machinations of which are a direct parallel to the Brexit shenanigans of the twenty-first century. Hampshire was the final attempt by Owen to build a Utopian community, the intended ultimate model upon which to base his 'New Moral World'.

---

1 Owen, Robert, *The Life of Robert Owen by Himself,* Beer, M. (ed.), (London 1920), p.xi.
2 *The Builder*, 28.10.1843, p.453.
3 Evinson, Denis, *Joseph Hansom* (unpublished Masters dissertation, University of London, 1966) and Allen, Clare Bridget, *Joseph Hansom Architect 1803-1882* (unpublished BA, Manchester University, 1977).

Introduction

There are difficulties with accuracy in this narrative. Theoretically older published sources such as Podmore should be authentic, but they sometimes conflict or are misleading when written out of context. Even Owen's newspaper entitled *New Moral World* was known to be heavily edited, and frequently distorted to reflect his personal opinions. The contemporary report of George Holyoake's visit to Harmony Hall lacks an element of background knowledge, and is based solely on his view of the premises as they stood at the time of his visit. Perhaps direct quotes are the nearest to reality, though even these are inevitably open to interpretation. This dilemma is compounded by the complexity of Owen's nature, the diversity of his activities, and his own self-contradictory views. Royle described him as delusionary.[4] On trawling through the more notable sources on Robert Owen's chaotic life, it becomes increasingly apparent that it is difficult to separate fact from fiction as they are inevitably embedded within multifarious interpretations. One aspect which is strikingly constant, is the huge aspirational scale of Owen's activities and the repeated use of superlatives. To give authenticity and vitalise the drama of events, the text is liberal with quotes, especially from contemporary writings. To paraphrase would risk misinterpretation. Thus it is hoped that the use of original wording adds clarity, whilst still leaving scope for independent analysis.

Acknowledgements and Sources

Grateful thanks must be given to the Co-operative College in Manchester and to the Robert Owen Museum in Newtown, both of which gave ready access to their archives; likewise Birmingham Archives and Special Collections and the Gladstone Library in Flintshire. Secondly, and most importantly, many texts have been accessed, without which this book would not have been possible. Each and every source has its own speciality, for Owen's life lends itself to so many different facets of the age in which he lived and shows how and why he tried to change them all. They range from the glorification and hagiography of McCabe, to overviews by Booth and Cole, with Podmore being traditionally recognised as the standard. Of the more specialised works, Davis and O'Hagan delve into educational aspects, whilst Royle attempts to 'demystify some of the myths associated with Owen' by giving a down-to-earth exploration into the finances at Harmony Hall. Centenaries and symposia, such as Edinburgh and Gregynog (Cole, Thompson and Williams) give the opportunity for fresh perspectives. There are, of course many others, some of which are embodied within the text. As titles invariably cite Robert Owen, sub-titles are used as short-form references. Whereas the diversity of literature produced both on

---
4 Royle, Edward, *Robert Owen and the Commencement of the millennium,* (Manchester, 1998), p.18, quoting Beer, *Life of Owen*, p.xxi.

and by Owen personifies his life, of Hansom little has been published. The obituary prepared by his youngest son, Joseph Stanislaus, focusses mainly on his architectural works, but Hansom's 'Statement of Facts', which chronicles his troubled times in Birmingham, together with several articles in *The Builder,* give some insight into his personal views.

Context
During the first half of the nineteenth century, Britain, England, and London in particular, were places of fear, with genuine apprehension as to a repeat of France's uprisings re-occurring on British soil. The aftermath of the French Revolution and the Napoleonic Wars had led to financial losses, instability and uncertainty. Discontent and unrest in Ireland were rife, alongside deep resentment at London's parliamentary control, for the Irish were as yet unrepresented and posed a serious threat to the *status quo.* This was one potential trigger factor. At a more local level, Birmingham too was affected. A pro-active town of diverse small industrial workshops, soon to become a hothead of religious and political dissent and a near rival to London, it was eager to benefit from the industrial revolution and, like the rest of the nation, it too suffered from loss of work. Men returned from the Napoleonic Wars with no jobs, and munitions production, a mainstay of industrial activity, was no longer required. This was a national phenomenon: money was short, the Corn Laws upset Ireland and the reformed Poor Laws were unpopular in England. It was against this backdrop that Owen and Hansom came together briefly to 'put the world to rights'.

In 1833, the peak of Owen and Hansom's collaboration, Owen was 62 years old, and Hansom was just half his age, at 31 years. Despite the age gap and the differences in their personalities, Owen and Hansom also had much in common, in particular their desire for better living conditions for the poor and improved education. Essentially they had strong and supportive family backgrounds, benefitted from schooling at an early age (not the norm, but in tune with Owen's subsequent belief that character is formed by the nature of the environment), and both had good luck in their formative years.[5] Owen followed his brother to London and thence to an apprenticeship in Lincolnshire, followed by a spell in Manchester, the centre of England's flourishing cotton trade, where he joined the prestigious Literary and Philosophical Society and acquired oratorical skills. Hansom's career started with the release of his apprenticeship by his builder-father, to a posting in Halifax where he gained much experience and then formed an independent partnership with Edward Welch. Owen and Hansom were both workaholics,

---

[5] Donnachie, Ian, *Robert Owen: Owen of New Lanark and New Harmony* (East Lothian, 2000), p.19; *The Builder,* 8 July 1882, p.44.

big travellers and dedicated to their individual causes. Where they differed was in that Owen was a very public person and relished in addressing large audiences. He also used his quickly gained wealth as leverage for his own self-promotion.[6] Hansom was similarly adept at networking, but more on a one-to-one basis and less commercially orientated.

In different ways, and for different reasons, Owen and Hansom were both described as pioneers, both products of their age, yet also ahead of times. However this book will demonstrate that the communities upon which Owen based his hopes for the future, were not the product of original thought. The much-used Biblical quote, that 'there is nothing new under the sun', is certainly apt in the case of Owen, for his first community at New Lanark, near Glasgow was built upon some of the traditions which had already been started by David Dale, his predecessor and future father-in-law. Furthermore, there was a simultaneous phase of community-building immediately after the massive social restructuring in France which took place following the Revolution of 1795, and again in Poland after the insurrection against Russia in 1830.[7]

Harrison concludes that Owenism was a cluster of ideas, contemporaneous with the time in which he lived.[8] What was unique to Owen was his all-encompassing belief that communities were the solution to social and economic problems on a global scale. He opined that the cause of unrest and discontent in British Society was that it lacked a 'sense of community', and aspired to the whole world becoming 'one enormous happy family'. Donnachie interprets the word 'happy' as meaning a more docile and compliant community, away from the current state of dissatisfaction and unrest.[9] Hansom did not entirely share Owen's approach, and his brief period of active participation in politics, when he first encountered Owen, came to an abrupt and cathartic end, when the execution of his design for the town hall in Birmingham resulted in bankruptcy. Nevertheless, his subsequent journal, *The Builder*, was used to voice concerns on social welfare, such as when the Metropolitan Buildings Act of 1844 was criticised.[10] Very much along the lines of Owen, he published an article entitled 'Treatment of Work-People by their Employers' in his trial precursor issue, see Chapter II. As for his profession, the constant soul-searching in the nineteenth century for a new style to represent the 'modern' age, was all to no avail. Unable to come up with anything new, architects were dragged back to former times, hence the Gothic Revival.

Again their views on the importance of education were similar but not the same. Owen claimed that 'to train and educate the rising generation will at all

---

6 Donnachie, *Owen of New Lanark*, p.21.
7 Bronowski, J. and Mazlish, Bruce, *The Western Intellectual Tradition* (London, 1960).
8 Harrison, J.F.C., *Robert Owen and the Owenites in Britain and America* (London, 1969), p.4.
9 Donnachie, *Owen of New Lanark*, p.166.
10 *The Builder,* 9 November 1844.

times be the first objective of society, to which all other will be subordinate'.[11] He was also convinced that ignorance was the cause of crime.[12] Hansom had a simple, more practical approach, believing that schooling should be a basic human right. They both hoped that education would lead to a more stable and better informed society, the one leading to the other. This appealed to many land-owning politicians with large business enterprises, who were concerned as to the level of unrest, and welcomed any ideas which might alleviate the situation. At times their support extended to generous donations. Whilst Owen was riding on the back of community living to realise his dreams, Hansom's approach was more pragmatic. Rather than trying to influence legislation, he took advantage of a number of Acts of Parliament which, in turn, provided him with work. Repatriation of English Catholics, forced to flee back to England during the Revolution, swelled the population and created a need for more churches. This was further aided by the Catholic Emancipation Act of 1829. His work then extended to self-sufficient Catholic communities, when convents and educational establishments were called for, not so far removed from Owen's ideals.

Synopsis
The lives of both Owen and Hansom exemplify Owen's strong conviction that character is founded on one's upbringing and surroundings. Owen was born in Newtown and Hansom in York, the significance of which will be portrayed in Chapters I and II respectively. To better understand how Hansom was able to contribute to Owen's master plan, to change the world and rid it of what in his view were perceived evils, these chapters start by exploring their respective earlier years. In Owen's case, emphasis will be placed on his time spent at New Lanark, near Glasgow, the first of his three communities. It will show how it was here that he developed his theories on the 'Formation of Character', and how he sought to transform future generations by conditioning small children from infancy, thus ensuring an improved adulthood, Owen's concept of a new millennium. It then moves to his time spent in America, an unfortunate episode which lost him much money. Touching briefly on Hansom's upbringing and the start of his professional career as an architect, the second chapter reveals his association with Owen and the radical mood which dominated Birmingham in the 1830s. This is developed further in the third chapter, where Owen's plans for monetary reform and Labour Notes are integrated with those of the banker and future politician Thomas Attwood. It shows how Owen returned to Birmingham to form Trades Unions, which led to strikes, disrupting Hansom's career yet again. Chapter IV investigates

---
11 Robert Owen, 'The Social System – Constitution, Laws, and Regulations of a Community', (1826).
12 Royle, *millennium,* p.50.

Introduction

Harmony Hall, Owen's final community, how it was set up and concluding that it never was going to be a success. It back-tracks to New Lanark and Owen's move to America showing that he misguidedly attempted to incorporate facets of his previous ventures into a new community, one which was in quite the wrong location and devoid of any meaningful funding. It is not clear at what stage Hansom's active involvement came to an end. Owen and Harmony Hall are cited in his obituary, but seldom is due credit given to the time and effort he devoted to what would have undoubtedly been one of his most outstanding enterprises, had it not been beleaguered by debt, conflict and a lack of clarity of purpose. However it is noticeable that when reporting on Hansom's lecture at the Reading Mechanics Institute, the writer carefully avoided mentioning that Hansom had been the architect of Harmony Hall.[13] The fifth chapter shows how George Edmondson, one of his benefactors in Lancashire, and also an early Birmingham connection of both Hansom and Owen were brought in as Harmony Hall (latterly Queenwood College) moved into an attempted recovery phase. By summarising their lives, the one after the other, it will be seen that there is a distinct dichotomy between their many similarities and their fundamental differences. Owen stuck rigidly to his theories throughout, whereas Hansom was more flexible and better able to adjust to and take advantage of changes.

To add clarity and enhance social context, a time line has been appended to the main script. Additionally short biographies elaborate upon information given in the body of the text, depicting a selection of key personalities and the contribution they made. Wherever possible, a 'likeness' has also been attached.

---

13 *Hampshire Chronicle* 16 August 1843; Garnett, Ronald George, *Co-operation and the Owenite socialist communities in Britain 1825-45* (Manchester, 1972), p.189.

CHAPTER I

ROBERT OWEN –

a man with a vision

EARLY YEARS

Family
Robert Owen was born in Wales. Typically described as the son of a saddler in Newtown, Montgomeryshire, his childhood was far more complex than that. He described Newtown as a small town of less than 1000 people, neat, clean and beautifully situated. His father was probably also an ironmonger, and certainly the local postmaster, responsible for overall management of local parish affairs. His mother was the daughter of 'one of the most respected local farmers'.[1] Beer claims that Owen's father lost an estate of the value of £500 due to mishandling by his father's lawyer, who had been bribed.

    The youngest but one of seven children, schooling for Owen started between the ages of four and five, when he learnt to read, write and perform basic arithmetical tasks. His favourite food was flummery, the Welsh equivalent to Scotch porridge. This made its impression on Owen when, in haste, as usual, he ate some which was so hot that it scalded his stomach leaving him with a perceived permanent eating disorder. However, this did

---
1 Beer, *Life of Owen*, p.1.

not prevent him from being wined and dined in his adult life any more than his teetotal views prevented him from keeping a well-stocked wine cellar at Braxfield, his Scottish home.[2] The family appeared to reside in the proximity of Newtown Hall, the residence of the eccentric Sir John Powell Price, Bart, and he received his schooling in or adjacent to the main house.[3] The hall was Jacobean, with many gables and much splendid carved panelling. It claimed a connection with Charles I, who had stayed there for two nights after the battle of Naseby.[4] This snippet of information goes some way to explain why Owen instinctively sought support from high-ranking personnel and was clearly comfortable in their company. As Owen was to proclaim on many an occasion, early upbringing was of profound importance. He was such a good pupil that he became assistant to his teacher, William Thickens (nick-named Mr Thickness), and was asked to assist with younger children.[5] A passion for reading developed when he was taken under the wing of three Methodist spinsters who lent him many books.

Throughout his life Owen was a prolific writer, though his works reflected his personality, demonstrating his tendency towards verbosity and repetition. However, when he created his school at New Lanark in Scotland, he preferred a more practical approach, using charts, plans and diagrams rather than text, with a minimal use of books, preferably not before the age of twelve. The greatest influence of these three ladies was to make him aware of the extent of animosity between different religions, so much so that he concluded that there was 'something fundamentally wrong in all religions'. His subsequent public proclamation to this effect at the London Tavern in August 1817 caused a considerable outcry and overshadowed his more favourable activities in a way which he could never quite shake off. Henry (Lord) Brougham, an ardent supporter who was present at the time, said 'How the devil could you say what you did yesterday at your public meeting? If any of us had said half as much we should have been burned alive, and here you are quietly walking [about] as if nothing had occurred'.[6]

What Owen's account of his early life tells us is that he was a precocious child with an enquiring mind and an inherent thirst for learning. There is nothing to suggest that he was put under any pressure to read, or indeed to investigate factory systems and other forms of education as he did later in life. What it does not explain is how he came to take such a strong, almost dictatorial approach when he tried to change the world from what he called the 'old ways' to the 'new ways'. A hint of his autocratic approach appears

---

2 Donnachie, *Owen of New Lanark*, p.7.
3 Beer, *Life of Owen*, p.2.
4 Podmore, Frank, *Robert Owen, a biography* (London, 1906, reprinted New York 1968), pp.4-5.
5 Claeys, Gregory, *Selected Works, Life, of Robert Owen*, p.52.
6 Booth, Arthur John, *Robert Owen, the founder of Socialism in England* (London, 1869), p.77.

when he stated that he asked [his mother] to ensure that his breakfast was always ready on time.

Training
His career escalated at a rapid pace right from a very early age. Leaving school at nine years, he moved to join his brother, also a saddler, in London. He remained there for just six weeks before moving to Stamford in Lincolnshire where he completed an apprenticeship to a draper.[7] He was only paid in terms of board and lodging for the first year, after which he was given eight pounds a week, and then ten pounds in his third year. It was fortuitous that James McGuffogg, his employer, had a large library. As work ended at four o'clock each day, that gave Owen a further opportunity to read. He remained pious at this stage and it was here that he relished the first taste of how he could influence others. Having written to Prime Minister William Pitt, encouraging him to pursue legislation regarding observance of the Sabbath, he attributed a subsequent notice in *The Times* to this effect as having been prompted by his letter. As McGuffogg and his wife had differing views on religion, Owen again began to question its impact, coming to the conclusion that this should more properly be replaced with a 'spirit of universal charity'.[8] During 1785, at the age of thirteen, Owen moved back to London briefly, from where he relocated to Manchester, seemingly headhunted by a large cotton mill, with a salary of £40 *per annum*.

Manchester
It was in Manchester that his career really took off. The town was rapidly expanding and was dubbed 'Cottonopolis' due to its devotion to the cotton industry. Owen borrowed £100 from his brother and, together with a colleague, they opened a new factory and employed forty men. Once again he was headhunted, this time becoming manager of a mill with five hundred workers and a salary of £300 *per annum*. Using his spare time to study the cotton industry, he turned down the offer of a partnership, which could have led to an improvement of salary to £500 *per annum*, and instead took on the post of managing director at the Chorlton Twist Company.[9] This was based in an eight-storey building constructed in 1795, two of the storeys being below ground. Along with success came a reputation and he became respected as a business man, so much so that he was invited to join the prestigious local Literary & Philosophical Society. This introduced him to the hitherto unknown world of debating, an invaluable skill which enabled him to speak effectively at mass meetings across the country and abroad. Not only was

---
7 McCabe, Joseph, *Robert Owen* (London, 1820), p.4.
8 McCabe, *ibid.*, p.5.
9 McCabe, *ibid.*, p.8.

Manchester a training ground professionally, but it was also an eye-opener, for Owen began to question the appalling living conditions of his workers, and concluded that man was moulded by his environment, which in turn led to vice and crime. The problem, as he saw it, was ignorance; and the solution was education.

Owen's work in the Lancashire mills necessitated considerable travel as he sought to investigate other factories and how they operated. It was whilst he was on one of these trips that he met and subsequently married the daughter of the founder and owner of a large complex of mills at New Lanark, near Glasgow. Owen could not have envisaged the extent to which his move to Scotland changed the direction of his life, and probably never realised that he owed this to one man, Richard Arkwright. In 1784 Arkwright, the inventor of the water-frame, was taken on a sight-seeing trip by the Glasgow merchant David Dale, to view the spectacular Falls of Clyde. Arkwright proclaimed that 'Lanark would probably become the Manchester of Scotland', that is to say the principal Scottish processor of cotton. In 1799 Owen, along with two Manchester partners, purchased New Lanark from Dale. He decided that it was not his intention to be a mere manager of cotton mills, but to change the conditions of the people.[10] In less than fifteen years, Owen had completely transformed it into a place much admired and visited by many distinguished visitors from all over Europe and America, including the future Tsar of Russia, and Queen Victoria's father, the Duke of Kent.

NEW LANARK

The situation in New Lanark as Owen found it comprised men, women and children working six days a week in foul, insanitary, badly-lit rooms from six in the morning until seven in the evening, though there is general consensus that Owen may have exaggerated. Children worked from the age of seven, and included batches of orphans routinely transferred from workhouses. McCabe describes the changes made by Owen in rather dramatic terms: from a place of 'thieving, lying, swearing, drinking, and fighting' to 'the happiest, healthiest, and most virtuous village of the civilised world'.[11] At first, even the workers, who were accustomed to their appalling conditions, resisted change. Owen was challenged: 'If your supreme command is that men shall be happy, on what grounds do you interfere with men who are happy in ignorance, drink, dirt, and sensualism?'[12]

Owen was a well-intentioned philanthropist, of that there is no doubt, and some of his measures were ahead of their time, but his carrot-and-stick regimen at New Lanark was also strict and unyielding. He devised what

---
10 Cole, G.D.H. (introduction Cole, Margaret) *Life,* p.56.
11 McCabe, *Robert Owen,* p.12.
12 McCabe, *ibid.,* p.14.

became known as a 'Bug Hunting' system to ensure that homes were kept clean and in good order. He also closed public houses, and a day's pay was docked from those who were found to be drunk on New Year's Eve.[13] In the work-place he instigated a rigorous checking system to prevent theft, and he introduced 'Silent Monitors', a means of assessing work performance.[14] These monitors were small pyramid-like blocks of wood hung above each worker, painted black, blue, yellow and white. They were rotated according to performance, black being the worst and white the best. Owen disapproved of punishment, both for his workers and for the children in his school, but nevertheless the monitor system must have had an underlying intention to humiliate those who were not performing adequately. Frequently away from New Lanark, when he was there Owen inspected the mills daily. As with thefts, work performance was recorded meticulously.

On the positive side, the site of Owen's mills became a living community as much as a place of work, a concept with which he was hitherto not intimately familiar, but one which was to become fundamental to fulfilling his ambition. It is, perhaps, for this reason that he described his communities as experiments. He improved working conditions, shortened working hours and organised on-site shops with greatly reduced prices, generally twenty-five per cent lower than those in town. He also founded a Sick Fund, though all workers were obliged to make a small financial contribution. There were no boundary walls as such, but the inhabitants were in effect entrapped within the community and more-or-less obliged to abide by Owen's rules and regulations. Owen was not averse to self-praise. He described New Lanark as 'the most important experiment for the happiness of the human race that had yet been instituted at any time in any part of the world'.[15] However when he was invited to sit for the modellers at Madame Tussaud's, her Jesuit advisor vetoed this, saying that he had no objection to her exhibiting murderers if she so wished, but not an infidel.[16]

Four Essays on the Formation of Character 1812

From 1812, Owen produced four essays on the principle of 'The formation of the human character, and the application of the principle to practice', each of which elaborated on previous versions. He started by emphasising the Formation of Character and worked his way through principles applied in practice to principles applied to Government. In his second essay he outlined

---

13 McCabe, *ibid.,* p.15.
14 Donnachie, *Owen of New Lanark,* pp.84, 85.
15 Davison, Lorna and Arnold, Jim, 'The Great Experiment: New Lanark from Robert Owen to World Heritage Site', p.56 quoting from the *Selected Works of Robert Owen* by Gregory Claeys (London, 1993), vol.4, p.112, in Thompson, Noel and Williams, Chris (ed.) in *Robert Owen and his Legacy* (Cardiff, 2011).
16 McCabe, *Robert Owen,* p.57.

his methodology and achievements at New Lanark, stating: 'I hesitate not to say that the members of my community may by degrees be trained to live *without idleness, without poverty, without crime,* and *without punishment,* for each of these is the effect of error in the various systems prevailing. They are all necessary consequences of ignorance'.[17] Here we begin to see repetition creeping in. Essay number three stressed the need for education to start at the earliest possible age, whilst the fourth essay demanded education for all and moves to a political scenario, stating that 'The end of government is to make the governed and the governors happy ... government is the best practice to produce the greatest happiness to the greatest number, *including those who govern and those who obey*' (author's italics). This seems to conflict with his overall philosophy but depicts him in dictatorial mode. His views on a classless society are also muddled as he both acknowledges and condemns capitalism. The essays were eventually combined in his *New View of Society* and sent to various high-profile people, such as The Prince Regent and William Wilberforce. A copy, addressed to his Friends and Countrymen was circulated amongst the general public.[18] These literary works culminated in the building of his Institution for the Formation of Character which opened on New Year's Day 1816 and housed his school.

Working conditions

A secondary but important area where Owen did achieve a measure of success was his campaign for factory reform. Though he contrived to improve working conditions in his New Lanark Mills, he was aware that they continued to be very poor elsewhere. Accompanied by his eldest son, Robert Dale Owen, Robert senior scoured the country, visiting the factories of others and assessing their work practices. His aim was to produce damning facts sufficient to pressurise government into introducing compulsory reforms which would reduce working hours, raise the minimum age for employing children, and provide some form of education.[19] In addition, he also believed in equal rights for men and women and wrote thus in the *New Moral World*: 'Women will be no longer made the slaves of, or dependent upon men ... They will be equal in education, right, privileges and personal liberty'. Employers resented Owen's interference and resisted change – they were only interested in profit and certainly did not welcome the notion of factory inspectors. As will be seen, the only action the employees could take was to withdraw their labour and come out on strike. This did not work because the vastly more-

---

17 See Garnett, *Co-operation,* p.5, n.44, *A New View of Society,* 1813, in *A View of Society and other writings,* p.37.
18 Gatrell, V.A.C. (ed.), Robert Owen's *A New View of Society and Report to the County of Lanark,* (New Lanark, 1813 – 1821).
19 Beer, *Life of Owen,* p.vi.

powerful employers turned upon the workers, depriving them of their income and locking them out of their factories.

A very practical aspect with which Owen grappled was the concept of machinery, an issue with which all parties were concerned. On the one hand it should both improve production (satisfying the employers), and reduce working hours (satisfying employees as fewer working hours would produce the same output), but on the other hand there were negative aspects. Employers were greedy. They controlled the inanimate machines and refused to acknowledge the on-going contribution made by workmen and, of course, their children, without whom profit would be severely diminished. Owen blamed this on competition, but his was a largely losing battle.[20] Machines, so favoured by mill masters, were also a contributory factor to domestic upheaval. They broke up families taking people away from home-based cottage industry and into large overheated, unhealthy and soul-destroying buildings of mass production.[21] During his subsequent visit to America, Owen contended that the conditions of English workers were far worse than those of slaves in the West Indies.[22] The slave trade was already an emotive subject, shortly to be described by Gladstone as 'burdonsome'.[23] It created a personal dilemma for Gladstone inasmuch as his father, his brother, and many of their associates, were slave owners. However, in 1833 he echoed Owen's views, saying that 'child employees [in England] were less well taken care of than many a slave'.[24]

It took several years of lobbying through Sir Robert Peel, a textile manufacturer and father of the future Prime Minister, before Owen was able to trigger the Factory Act of 1819. It was a significant milestone, but the measures were slow to come into effect and did not go anywhere as far as he had hoped. His plea for education was completely ignored. In 1815 he had already distributed copies of his 'Observations on the Effects of the Manufactory System' to every member of parliament and peer of the realm. The purpose of the pamphlet was twofold, it was also an instrument of self-promotion, a way of bringing his name to the attention of the recipients.[25] He then drafted a bill aiming to reduce the working hours of adults to twelve hours (less one and a half for meals), with no children under the age of ten, and then only working a six-hour day. Bills were passed in 1825, 1833 and again in 1847, but the ten-hour working day was not formalised until 1847.

---
20 Butt, John, 'Robert Owen and Trade Unionism', in 'Robert Owen, Industrialist, Reformer, Visionary 1771-1858', p.16.
21 For a graphic description of conditions in Preston, see Leigh, J.S., *Preston Cotton Martyrs: The millworkers who shocked a nation* (Lancaster, 2008).
22 Donnachie, *Owen of New Lanark*, p.122.
23 Foot, M.R.D. (ed.), *The Gladstone Diaries* (Oxford, 1978) I, p.52, quoting 3 August 1833.
24 Stansky, Peter, *Gladstone: A Progress in Politics* (New York and London, 1979), p.28.
25 Donnachie, *Owen of New Lanark*, p.123.

Education

The feature for which New Lanark is most noted is education, the first ever school for infants, the equivalent of today's pre-school nurseries; general schooling for older children; and evening lectures and concerts for the older population. Owen was convinced that bad habits were ingrained from birth, and wanted children to attend his nursery school almost as soon as they could walk – but everything was amusement, they were 'not to be annoyed with books'.[26]

This was an idea which had already been mooted by Johann Pestallozzi in Switzerland in 1805, though Owen would not have known about it at this stage. In this way he was hoping to produce a new and enlightened generation for the long-term future. 'It is in the interest of all, that every one, from birth, should be well educated, physically and mentally that society may be improved in its character'.[27] Other prerequisites were a good, natural environment, a healthy diet and plenty of fresh air, for in order to 'preserve permanent good health, the state of mind must also be taken into consideration'. Taking this a stage further, he thought that if people lived in villages or open parts of a town, this would be much better for their well-being than if they lived in crowded towns.[28]

By using New Lanark as an exemplar (or experiment), Owen attempted to tackle the problem by taking a bottom up approach. He was convinced that by leaving education, or training as he invariably put it, any later in life would mean that children were conditioned in ERROR, implying that it would be difficult to undo bad habits.[29] Owen's ideals of education being pleasurable were not approved of by everyone. Nevertheless, the school was a great success, with children and parents alike seeming happy, and numerous distinguished guests impressed. Classes were usually of between thirty and fifty children, and lessons were informal with children roaming around, not sitting in rows. They learnt by observation and experience, contributing interactively with teachers, more like discussions or conversations than lessons, and wore simple, specially designed white tunics or sometimes kilts, and no shoes. Reading, writing and arithmetic were taught from the age of ten, but no learning was undertaken by rote, and preferably no books before the age of twelve. A large globe and maps of the world were important features, as was world history from a social point-of-view (not just lists of dates), and botany classes reflecting Owen's love of nature. The knowledge this imparted must have bemused the parents who knew nothing of life beyond their long working day in the mills.

---

26 Donnachie, *ibid.*, p.166.
27 Owen, Robert, 'A Development of the Principle & Plans on which to establish self-supporting Home Colonies', (1841).
28 Briggs, Asa, *Victorian Cities*, p.48.
29 Beer, *Life*, pp.288-289.

Owen set out ten 'commandments' which he felt were essential for a well-formed character. In summary: no punishment; unceasing kindness; instruction by the inspection of realities; questions to be answered in a kind manner; no regular indoor hours; music and military discipline; visits to gardens and orchards; training to think rationally; and time spent in superior surroundings.[30] Emphasis was always on group activities, and children were encouraged to be kind to each other.

City of London Tavern

Much of the year after Owen opened his Institution was spent in London. It was here that he delivered two notable addresses, firstly on communities, and then, as already mentioned, the one which referred to his views on religion. Though diverting in part from his central themes of 'formation of character' and education, he used these as an opportunity to counter the rebuffs he had just received when he tried to launch his fantastical 'Plan' as outlined on page 28. Owen's choice of venue is a reflection of the importance he attributed to the message he was trying to put across. The City of London Tavern was a large, impressive building in Bishopsgate, with a dining room decorated with Corinthian columns and popular for both public and private meetings, mainly supporting political or charitable causes. Travelling, or at least spending time in London, was probably the cause of Owen's failure to win a seat in parliament. He lost the seat in the bi-election for Lanark and Linlithgow by four votes, and lost again in the subsequent general election.[31]

Owen always went to considerable trouble to publicise his meetings, ensuring that they were well attended. The power of the press was a phenomenon of the Victorian age, symptomatic of the speeding up of society and the industrial revolution. Wolff and Fox saw it as making greater impact than even the increase in population.[32] Owen's printing costs are incalculable. He purchased and circulated 30,000 copies of newspapers which summarised his proposals, sending them to 'every parish minister, members of both Houses of Parliament, chief magistrates and bankers, and one to each of the leading persons in all classes'.[33] Apart from his own many newspapers, which were subsidised by the branches, he used every other conceivable opportunity to publicise his theories. This was continuous throughout his life, not only with his Four Essays and his Report at New Lanark, which were translated into French and German, and his newspapers *The Crisis, The Pioneer* but especially *New Moral World*. He also distributed 60,000 pamphlets at the Great Exhibition in Hyde Park in 1851, again translated into French and

---

30 Beer, *ibid.,* pp.318-319.
31 McCabe, *Robert Owen,* p.54.
32 Wolff, Michael and Fox, Celina, 'Pictures from the Magazines' in Dyos & Wolff, *Victorian City,* p.559.
33 Donnachie, *Owen of New Lanark,* p.138; Booth quotes the number as 40,000, Booth, *Socialism,* p.76.

German, and ultimately published his *Millennium Gazette* which ran from 1856 through to his dying days.

The first of the two 1817 meetings in particular was part of an expensive publicity campaign, with an audience of twelve hundred people.[34] He commenced with a condemnation of the capitalist system and ended with a case for the setting up of self-sufficient communities, or Villages of Unity and Mutual Co-operation. These were the two most important talks of his career – the venue, the number and profile of people attending and the impact they made – or not in the case of the communities. Reports of this meeting were so numerous that they delayed every mail coach from London by twenty minutes.[35] In addition to his lengthy rhetoric, Owen produced excessively detailed plans and set out his considered estimate of costs, as shown below. Bearing in mind that this referred to a single village community, it is not surprising that those he was trying to convince were deterred by the total figure of £96,000 (more than five and a half million pounds as of 2017). Nevertheless, Owen claimed that, based on families of two adults and two children, together with superintendents, clergymen, schoolmasters and surgeons, this worked out at £4 per head, and was cheaper than the Poor Law system.

SCHEDULE OF EXPENSES FOR FORMING AN
ESTABLISHMENT FOR 1,200 MEN, WOMEN AND CHILDREN
If the land be purchased.

1,200 acres of land at £30 per acre	36,000
Lodging apartments for 1,200 persons	17,000
Three public buildings within the square	11,000
Manufactory, slaughter-house, and washing house	8,000
Furnishing 300 lodging-rooms at £8 each	2,400
Furnishing kitchen, schools, and dormitories	3,000
Two farming establishments, with corn mill and malting and brewing appendages	5,000
Making the interior of square and roads	3,000
Stock for the farm under spade cultivation	4,000
Contingencies and extras	6,600

When his Plan was dismissed by the Archbishops' Committee, they referred him to the House of Commons Committee on the Poor Law, which also dismissed it. Owen took matters into his own hands and persuaded *The Times* to publish five columns on the topic.

---

34 Cole, Margaret, *Robert Owen of New Lanark* (London, 1953), p.91.
35 Donnachie, *Owen of New Lanark*, p.39.

Pestalozzi

Following the negative response to his outbursts in London, and with neither side willing to negotiate let alone compromise, Owen ventured to explore Europe, where his reputation as an educationalist, manufacturer and social thinker had preceded him. This was largely due to Lord Sidmouth, the Home Secretary who opposed Catholic Emancipation and widely circulated two hundred 'superiorly bound and interleaved' copies of his *New View of Society*.[36] Owen was accompanied by the Swiss Professor Charles de Rochemont Pictet, a statesman, diplomat and devotee who had recently visited New Lanark. Though he could not speak French, Owen was given an impressive array of introductions, in Paris, Geneva and finally Switzerland. He was even introduced to the French Prime Minister and invited to a banquet organised by Nathan de Rothschild.[37]

One of the highlights of his European tour was his sojourn at the newly founded Hofwyl Institute, built by Philipp Emanuel von Fellenberg near Bern in Switzerland. Fellenberg was a proponent of the Pestalozzi system, but he and Johann Heinrich Pestalozzi were not in sufficient accord to form a joint venture and a break-away establishment was set up at nearby Yverdon. Nevertheless, Pestalozzi greatly influenced Owen's thinking on education, especially his motto of 'learning by head, heart and hands', with child-focussed teaching rather than teacher-focussed. He also believed in the freedom of the child, the use of natural objects as teaching aids, a regimen of physical exercise and outdoor activity, and crucially 'that every aspect of the child's life contributed to the formation of their personality, character and capacity to reason'.[38] Owen and Fellenberg had much in common and Owen was so impressed with what he saw, and this, together with the international reputation it had gained, persuaded him to send his two eldest sons, Robert Dale aged sixteen years and William aged fourteen there to complete their education, by way of a 'finishing school'. They were the institute's first English pupils and, like their father, could speak no foreign languages, but were accepted because they had already received 'good private training and education, due to well-selected governors and tutors'.[39] The objectives of the founder were to cater for the poor, to provide a secondary school for local students, and to provide an institute for the sons of wealthy families. Fees were very expensive, yet it was in this latter bracket that Owen placed his sons, an example of Owen's double standards which calls into question his views on equality. His two younger sons were also sent there.[40] If he was truly the

---

36 Cole, *Robert Owen*, p.127.
37 Cole, *ibid.*, p.129.
38 See www.jhpestalozzi.org.
39 Beer, *Life*, pp.246-247.
40 Cole, *Robert Owen*, p.148.

'father of socialism', should his children not have been through the schooling system at New Lanark along with the others?

On returning to England, Owen temporarily abandoned his communities and focussed on two missions, education and factory reform. He was aware of official attempts to improve education by two proponents, Joseph Lancaster an educator and friend of his partner and manager, William Allen, and Dr Andrew Bell, a Scottish clergyman. Notwithstanding his own plans, he was magnanimous enough to offer £1,000 to each of them. Through his British and Foreign Schools Society, Lancaster supported the monitorial system of which Owen so disapproved, whereby older children instructed their juniors. Lancaster found this an expedient and effective means of teaching large numbers of poor children. Owen's offer to Bell was reduced to £500 when, as a supporter of the Church of England, Bell refused to offer his education to all denominations, in other words dissenters.

Report to the County of Lanark – 1820

Leading on from this, Owen was commissioned to produce his master 'Plan' in similar format to the Report which he had previously presented to the County of Lanark. In typical Owen style, the plan was given the lengthy title:

> 'For relieving Public Distress and Removing Discontent, by giving permanent, productive Employment to the Poor and Working Classes, under Arrangement which will essentially improve their Character, and ameliorate their Condition, diminish the Expenses of Production and Consumption, and create Markets coextensive with Production'.

The exposition he presented was very detailed and precise. It advocated the setting up of Villages of Unity and Co-operation, comprising between 500 and 1,500 people on plots of between 1,000 and 1,500 acres. Blocks of houses were to be laid out in large squares, with communal buildings in between. When this scheme was re-presented at the London Tavern, William Cobbett was scathing – he accused Owen of promoting 'parallelograms of paupers' or 'communities of slaves' as a means of controlling labour.[41] In Cobbett's words, Owen was:

> for establishing innumerable *communities* of paupers. Each is to be resident in an *enclosure* somewhat resembling a barrack establishment, only more extensive ... I perceive that they are all to be under a very *regular* discipline; and that wonderful peace, happiness and national benefit are to be the result.[42]

---

41 Donnachie, *Owen of New Lanark*, p.139.
42 Cobbett, *Political Register*, 1817, p.243.

A Committee was formed, of which Owen's supporters the Duke of Kent, Robert Peel and the economist David Ricardo, were members. However subscriptions were not sufficiently forthcoming and nothing came of it. England was a very religious country at this time and it is likely that Owen scuppered his own Plan with his misplaced reference to the adverse influence of religion, but the Plan did not die. It was resuscitated on several occasions.

William Allen

When Owen first arrived at New Lanark, he dismissed the existing managers as they didn't agree with his methods, even though one of them was Dale's half brother.[43] However, he didn't always get his own way. Owen, too, was dismissed as manager in 1812 and had to weave his way through financial contortions in order to purchase the property from his then partners and co-trustees following the death of Dale.[44] Having successfully acquired the property, his absence and constant travels left him vulnerable and eventually he had to leave both New Lanark and his subsequent New Harmony in the hands of others, firstly William Allen and then William Maclure. They both ultimately took over and developed what Owen had started in their own way, rather than following their predecessors' ideas.

Together with Jeremy Bentham, the radical utilitarian philosopher, Allen was one of six partners who re-purchased New Lanark in 1814, following the dissolution of the original partnership. Financial arguments had ensued over the settlement of Owen's late father-in-law's affairs and at one stage there was uncertainty as to New Lanark's future, potentially even leading to Owen's bankruptcy.[45] Allen's background was very different from that of Owen. The eldest son of a Quaker silk manufacturer, his former career had been as a chemist. He also had interests in agriculture and advocated self-sufficient settlements (or communities) which may have been what drew him to Owen's ideas. This combined with his interest in education and his leaning towards equality for women boded well for his initial interest in New Lanark. However, their differing views on religion, which Owen reiterated on many occasions, were the cause of irreconcilable ructions between Owen and Allen, ructions which eventually led to Owen's departure and his move to America. Owen was unable to mould Allen to his own ideals, described him as a 'busy, bustling, meddling' character and complained that Allen's 'mind was limited to Quaker prejudices'.

Like Owen, Allen also undertook extensive visits to Europe, and met various heads of state, including the Emperor of Russia, the king of Bavaria and the

---

43 Royle, *millennium*, p.13.
44 Royle, *ibid.*, p.12.
45 Donnachie, *Owen of New Lanark*, pp.105, 107.

king and queen of Spain.[46] On his return he started to fuel ill-feeling towards Owen and his condemnation of religion. Owen was more tolerant than some reports suggest; it was his cavalier way of expressing himself which caused such offence. As a Quaker, Allen objected to Owen's use of music, dance and military exercise, as well as drawing. This increased the rift between the two men. The military exercise, or drilling, was one of the physical activities Owen included for the children, for girls as well as for boys. He did not consider this to be aggressive, but more as something useful should a need for defence arise. No doubt this was influenced by recent events in France, but it was serious stuff, involving the use of fire-arms 'of proportionate weight and size to the age and strength of the boys [and girls] … who were to be taught complicated military movements'.[47] That his Quaker partners objected, is hardly surprising. However, one further thing to which Allen strongly objected was the form of costume worn, which allowed for naked legs.[48]

In Owen's absence, Allen had brought in a teacher from London and banned the dancing/singing/military exercises. As the chief financial backer of New Lanark, he turned out to be the more dominant of the two, for, following a management meeting in London, he wrote to Owen saying 'at present, it is quite plain to me that we must part'.[49] Owen sought to struggle on by encouraging high-profile visitors from overseas, with twenty thousand names entered in the visitor's book over period of ten years. One of his visitors was William Maclure, the Scottish geologist from Ayr who had spent several years compiling a geological survey of the United States single-handedly.[50] His visit was quickly followed by one from George Flower, the high-powered agent of the Rappite community in Indiana commissioned to dispose of 'Harmonie'.[51] This gave Owen an escape route – the opportunity to purchase a substantial and financially sound community. His exploits in America were a fascinating interlude, though disastrous financially. He arrived a rich man and left as a pauper.

NEW HARMONY

With matters clearly falling apart at New Lanark, the American settlement called 'Harmonie' had great appeal, especially the enormous scale of the project: 20,000 acres, 180 buildings and accommodation for 700 people.[52] Blinded by the cheap cost, roughly £25,000 compared with English estimates of three or four times that amount, together which what seemed to be a ready-

---

46 Beer, *Life*, p.324
47 Cole, *Owen of New Lanark*, p.85.
48 Jones, Lloyd, *The Life, Times, and Labours of Robert Owen*, vol.1, (London, 1890), p.119.
49 Davis and O'Hagan, *Robert Owen*, p.50; Jones, *Life, Times and Labours*, p.120.
50 Podmore, *biography*, p.299.
51 Harvey, Rowland Hill, *Robert Owen: social idealist* (Berkeley and Los Angeles, 1949), p.94.
52 Donnachie, *Owen of New Lanark*, p.215.

made income from pre-existing enterprises, Owen naively rushed into signing a contract. It comprised several factories and mills, dyeworks, a brickyard and a smithy, a tannery, a vineyard with distillery and stores, producing all the food and clothing necessary for the community, plus a church – a perfect setting for an experimental co-operative community, bigger and more diverse than New Lanark and free from English prejudices which Owen believed to have held him back. His self-conviction was such that he wrote to Allen stating 'For years past everything seems to have been preparing in an unaccountable and most remarkable manner for my arrival'.[53]

'Harmonie', later to be called New Harmony, was owned and led by George Rapp, a former German Lutheran priest who had been banned from his home country due to his radical ideas. The Rappites were devoted to the belief held by their founder, that is the New Coming around the time of the Commencement of the Millennium. Rapp now wished to return to his previous location in Pennsylvania, which he believed to be more lucrative. Despite warnings that the site might not be ideal, Owen did not stop to investigate this aspect. Rapp gave Owen an extensive tour of his village and its surroundings, but his mind was already made up. Having taken over, and with Robert Dale looking after his father's affairs at New Lanark, Owen left New Harmony in the hands of his second son William and Captain Donald Macdonald, the convert who had accompanied Owen on his initial inspection.

Things did not go according to plan and it was not long before the village began to deteriorate. The original village, under Rapp's leadership, had been run in a totally different way from New Lanark, the culture of the people was very different and the new incumbents were unwilling to adapt. They were more interested in working outside and didn't take to classroom teaching. Much to the annoyance of his father, William tried to be more selective and reduce the number of people who wanted to move there. Owen wanted the community to be open to all-comers, saying that 'a co-operatively designed environment would make settlers co-operative'.[54] But William had no choice – New Harmony was overflowing. At first there was sufficient food but there was a shortage of housing, with typically two or three families in the same dwelling. Many of Rapp's followers had relocated with him and new residents were people who either did not have appropriate skills or were not suited to community life. Realising this, Owen back-tracked to a simpler scheme and announced his 'Constitution of the Preliminary Society'. However, he was always impatient and soon reverted to his former ideals. Instead of remaining to build a rapport and establish a more solid foundation, he embarked upon a lengthy period of campaigning across America, giving talks and meeting

---
53 Letter Robert Owen to William Allen, 21 April 1825.
54 Ashe, Geoffrey, *The Offbeat radicals: the British tradition as alternative dissent* (London, 2007), p.98.

yet more men of influence who he hoped would become benefactors. As time went on, the Preliminary Society ran into debt due to consumption exceeding production, in part due to the cheap prices in the store which attracted non-communitarians.[55]

On his way back to Indiana Owen stopped off at Washington, where he exhibited a 6-foot square model of a self-contained city, the workings of which he explained to the President. The model was created by Thomas Stedman Whitwell, the architect and painter from New Lanark who had also accompanied Owen on his first trip and then became an art teacher at New Harmony. The intention was for it to be constructed three miles south of the existing village, but it was never built. Still scouring the world for ideas and glamourised by the company he had met on his European tour, together with those he had encountered on his journey from England, Owen became even more unrealistically ambitious. He gathered together a group of wealthy, élite academics and managed to persuade them to move with him to Indiana. Collecting people along they way, they joined him on a keelboat down the River Ohio, which became known as Owen's 'Boatload of Knowledge'. The boat was named 'Philanthropist'. Amongst his fellow travellers were William Maclure, the distinguished scientists Thomas Say and Charles Lesueur, the mineralogist Gerard Troost and the French Pestalozzi teacher, Marie Duclos Fretageot.[56] Charles Burgess described the group as 'The Boatload of Trouble', a truism as things worked out, yet he blames New Harmony's failure on Owen's abysmal record of mismanagement.[57] He wondered how Owen had managed to recruit Maclure, but Maclure had his own plans and was already committed following his visit to New Lanark, it was the gullibility of the others which is the more puzzling. There were plenty of younger children for Mme Fretageot, but where were the older children with higher skills, such as William and Robert Dale when they had been admitted to the school in Switzerland? They were few in number and largely imported, such as the children of Neef, the failed priest turned teacher. Thomas Say was the most popular, but Neef, a veteran of the Napoleonic wars, was considered very strict. A short rhyme satirised the situation:

> number 2 pigs locked up in a pen
> when they get out, it's now and then;
> when they get out, they sneak about,
> for fear old Neef will find them out.[58]

---

55 Donnachie, *Owen of New Lanark*, p.235.
56 Donnachie, *ibid.,* p.232.
57 Burgess, Charles, 'The Boatload of Trouble: William Maclure and Robert Owen Revisited', *Indiana Magazine of History,* XCIV, June 1998.
58 Wilson, William E., *The Angel and the Serpent, the story of New Harmony* (Indiana, 1984)

When William tried to teach the local children, he described his pupils as 'rough, boisterous, lawless … impatient of discipline and social restraints of any kind'.[59]

A study of the Rappites in America explains much about the way Owen tried to develop Harmony Hall. It explains why he tried to divide it into departments, his views on marriage, celibacy, why he carved CM 1841 above the door and why he attempted to grow grapes, an enterprise about which Holyoake was so scathing. The heated wall at Tytherley was estimated to have cost a guinea a yard, and grapes 'mortal few'.[60] As to the departments, as each was appointed its own head, this gave Owen an opportunity to shirk responsibility.

Owen's enthusiasm far outstretched his management capabilities and his more experienced recruits were shortly to become his successors. Owen had no clear idea as to how New Harmony was to be run, especially the financial side which was undeniably hazy. He hadn't even clarified in his own mind whether the villagers were to be employers, almsmen, partners or tenants.[61] This lack of clarity was a contributory factory to the diverse range of people who attempted to join. William Maclure, a devotee and financial backer of Pestalozzianism, shared many of Owen's beliefs but was sceptical about the abilities of the new people who had joined the community. He felt the only way forward was for education 'to be the chief support and foundation of the system'.[62] This was the final outcome, for Maclure soon took charge. It was hardly Owen's idea of spade cultivation, nor New Lanark-type cotton mills, but it suited his sons well, enabling them to build on the academic education they had undertaken in Switzerland, and leading to senior positions later in life.

The community suffered from drunkenness, theft and poor lodgings. The farms were not producing enough and Owen had to subsidise the village to keep it afloat. Socially it was a success, with dances, musical events and lectures, but The Preliminary Society failed financially and was reconstituted under the banner of a 'Community of Equality'.[63] This was formalised with a constitution and the equivalent of a management committee. The prime aim of the community was to promote happiness, by means of the following objectives:

---

59 Podmore, *biography*, p.14.
60 Holyoake, George, J., 'A Visit to Harmony Hall', published in *The Movement* (November 1844), p.9.
61 Donnachie, *Owen of New Lanark*, p.219.
62 Donnachie, *ibid.*, p.223 (76).
63 Donnachie, *ibid.*, p.236.

REVISED CONSTITUTION

Equality of rights, uninfluenced by sex or condition, in all adults.
Equality of duties, modified by physical and mental conformation.
Co-operative union, in the business and amusements of life.
Community of property.
Freedom of speech and action.
Sincerity in all our proceedings.
Kindness in all our actions.
Courtesy in all our intercourse.
Order in all our arrangement.
Preservation of health.
Acquisition of knowledge.
The practice of economy, or of producing and using the best of everything in the most beneficial manner.
Obedience to the laws of the country in which we live.[64]

It is noticeable that his 'Formation of Character' is no longer mentioned, and though by December 1825 there were 140 children boarded, education appears to be a low priority. Owen's personal mission developed along the lines of equality. However, even this failed as the social events were in themselves divisive, with a distinct lack of integration. When he told a young, delicately brought up girl to stop playing the piano and to go and milk the cows, was this Owen's idea of equality?[65] Josef Neef, one of his Pestalozzi teachers, accused Owen of having created a 'feudal barony'.[66] Far from being a hero, his strict rules, where the village, as foreseen by Cobbett, became more like an army barracks than a community, made him unpopular. There was a rigid routine, heralded by bells, such as at New Lanark, and a similar weekly work monitoring system, though without the wooden symbols. Macdonald left, disillusioned, as did Whitwell, the designer of his model. Even Robert Dale was beginning to lose faith.[67] Owen's salary from New Lanark was withdrawn and Rapp demanded money which was still outstanding. As he ploughed more and more of his capital into the project, Owen became aware that his financial situation was precarious. In an attempt to reinforce his status, he misguidedly came near to repeating his two disastrous talks from the London Tavern, using the American 4th July (1826) celebration to deliver a speech entitled 'Declaration of Mental Independence'.[68] He referred to

---

64 *New Harmony Gazette,* 15 February 1826.
65 Harrison, *Owen and the Owenites,* p.190.
66 Donnachie, *Owen of New Lanark,* p.243.
67 Donnachie, *ibid.,* p.244.
68 Donnachie, *ibid.*

evils inflicted upon the [human] race, and condemned private ownership of property, irrational systems of religion and marriage, inflammatory points of view not only for New Harmony, but also sending shock waves across the whole nation.

A new phase began when Owen tried to raise money by leasing 900 acres to Maclure for a School or Education Society, with Owen managing the rest of the village. Maclure moved into Rapp's former home and his new establishment became known as 'Macluria'.[69] The house was large and made of red brick – most of the residents lived in log cabins. Ostensibly to raise capital, this move was as much as anything due to their irreconcilable religious differences. At Maclure's suggestion, the whole population was then divided into departments, or communities. Initially there were three: his School or Education Society, an Agricultural and Pastoral Society, and a Mechanic and Manufacturing Society. These were then sub-divided according to function. Numerous attempts were made in quick succession to reorganise the community, as each one failed. Once again disagreements arose, particularly between Owen and Maclure. There were boundary disputes, and Owen, who had lost all the money he brought from Scotland, was left with no choice but to return to England, leaving behind his sons and one daughter.

---

[69] Harvey, *social idealist*, p.117.

1. Old Newtown

2. Robert Owen memorial, Newtown

3. Old New Lanark

4. New Lanark School House

5. *Dancing class by G. Hunt*

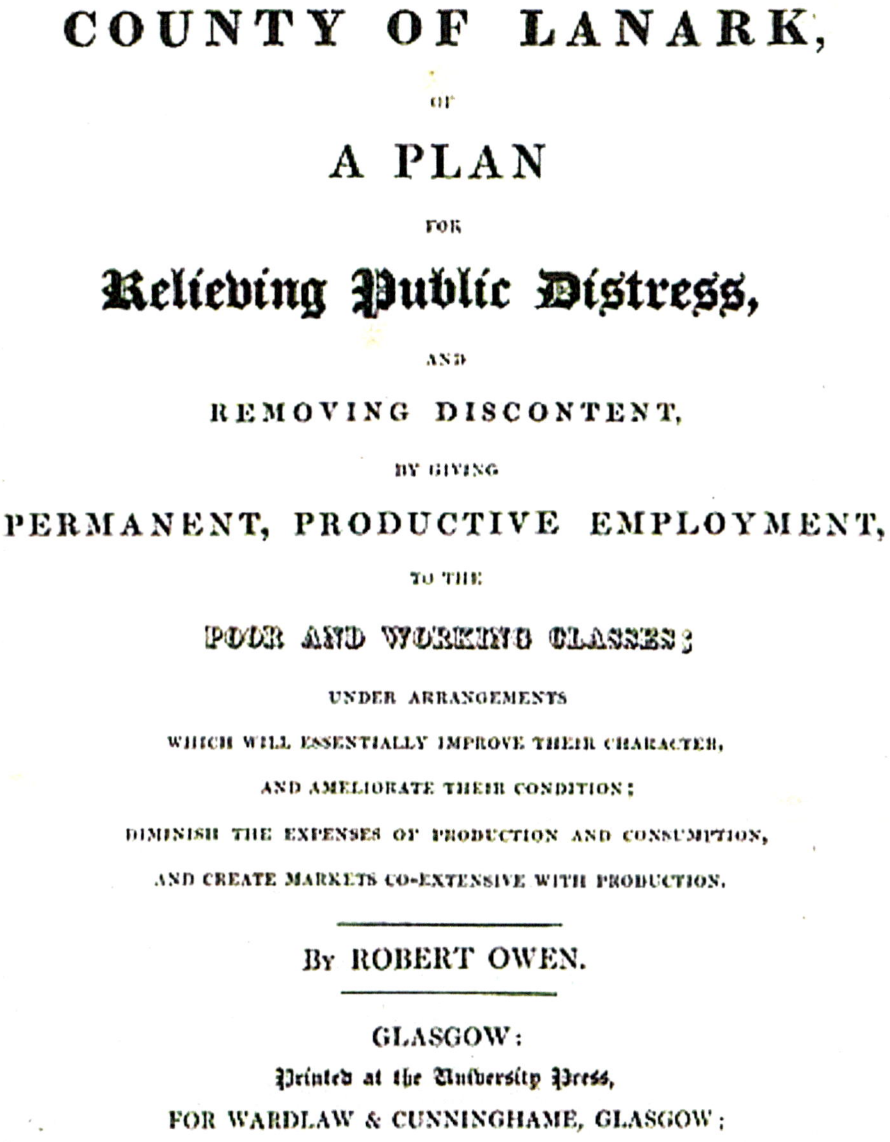

COUNTY OF LANARK,

OR

A PLAN

FOR

Relieving Public Distress,

AND

REMOVING DISCONTENT,

BY GIVING

PERMANENT, PRODUCTIVE EMPLOYMENT,

TO THE

POOR AND WORKING CLASSES;

UNDER ARRANGEMENTS

WHICH WILL ESSENTIALLY IMPROVE THEIR CHARACTER,

AND AMELIORATE THEIR CONDITION;

DIMINISH THE EXPENSES OF PRODUCTION AND CONSUMPTION,

AND CREATE MARKETS CO-EXTENSIVE WITH PRODUCTION.

By ROBERT OWEN.

GLASGOW:

Printed at the University Press,

FOR WARDLAW & CUNNINGHAME, GLASGOW;

CONSTABLE & CO., BELL & BRADFUTE, MANNERS & MILLER, AND WAUGH & INNES, EDINBURGH;

LONGMAN & CO., CADELL & DAVIES, JOHN MURRAY, AND

6. Owen's Plan

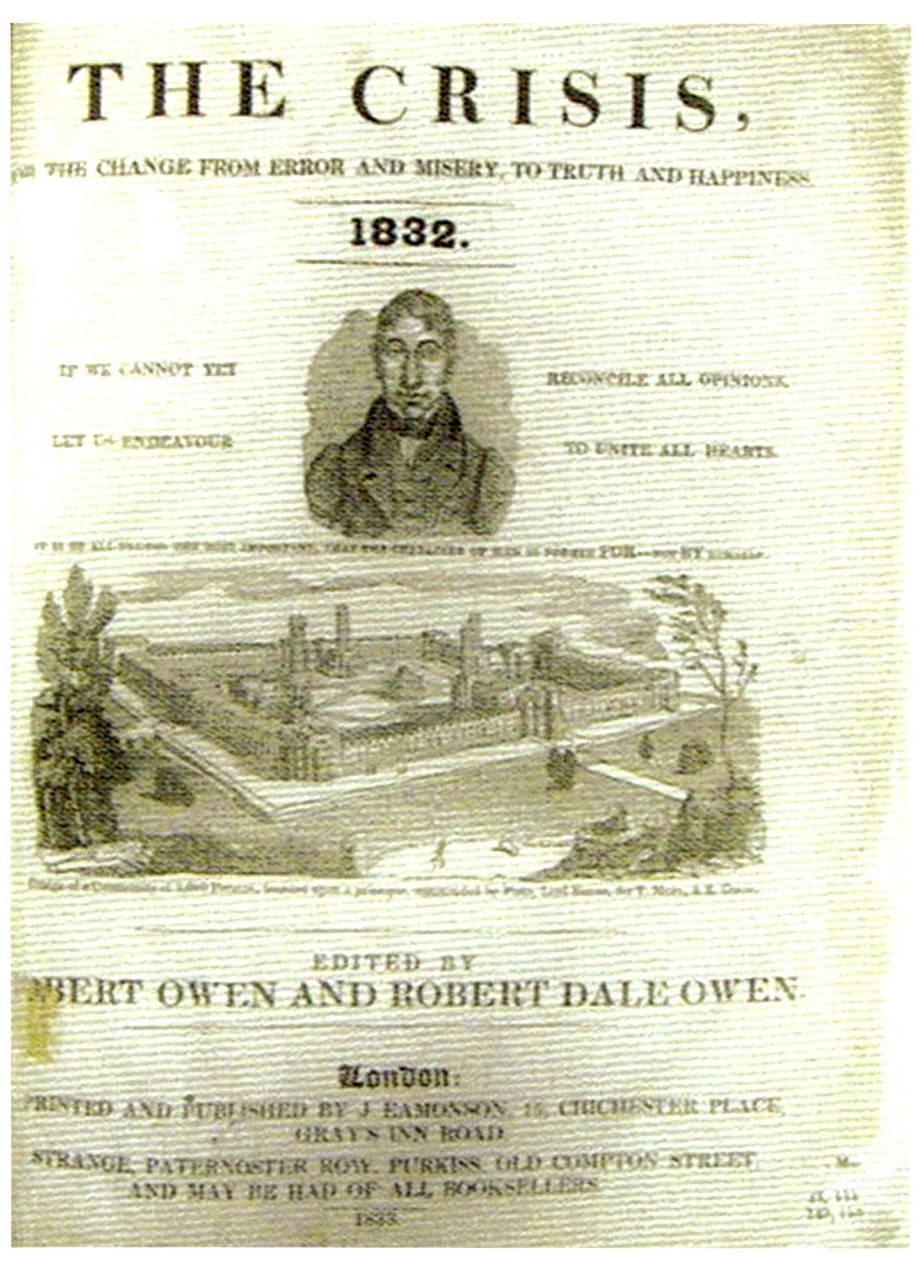

7. *The Crisis 1832*

CHAPTER II

JOSEPH HANSOM –

an architect with a social conscience

EARLY YEARS
Hansom was the second eldest of ten children. The family was well-established in York, where his father had been a Freeman of the City.[1] When Hansom was born, York was the sixteenth largest city in England, with a population of 16,846 and relatively unaffected by the Industrial Revolution. Micklegate, his birthplace, was one of the main entry points leading to the centre of the city – a prestigious street of diverse occupations. Their home was backed by stables converted into a workshop from which his father operated. Hansom left school at the age of thirteen, but went on to teach in night school, enhancing his own learning whilst assisting others. In his obituary, written by his youngest son Joseph Stanislaus Hansom, he was described as one of those men 'who never lost an opportunity of improving his mind, and would take up and study the most abstruse subject'. Of his character Joseph Stanislaus

---
1 This was a hereditary role which had been held by the Hansoms since 1724, and carried with it administrative functions and various privileges.

said that though his father held strong views, he was full of kindness and gentleness.[2] Hansom's upbringing gives some credibility to Owen's idea that early environment makes a great impact on adulthood. His childhood in York was hugely influenced by proximity to York Minster. The impression it made remained with him and he designed excessively large rose windows of the same size as the Minster in four of his future churches.[3]

Like Owen, Hansom was firstly apprenticed, to his builder-father, who acknowledged his talents and released him for architectural training. At this time the profession of architecture did not exist in any formal way and it was usual to be placed in the office of an established architect, in this case Matthew Phillips. On the untimely early death of Phillips he transferred to Halifax, where he worked for John Oates. This was an important turning point. Firstly he experienced working with the new Government-funded Commissioners Churches, and secondly he met Edward Welch, his future partner.[4] An unsuccessful application for the post of Surveyor of the Works in York proved fortuitous because this set him upon his travels around the country, seeking work, making contacts and gaining experience. As Evinson pointed out, Hansom's life was characterised by his acknowledgement of change and how he was 'prepared to consistently move with the times'.[5] Hansom and Welch were working simultaneously in Liverpool and on the Isle of Anglesey when the competition for the design of Birmingham Town Hall was announced in *The Times*. Hansom was so excited at the prospect that he declared that 'he would have it'. A premium of £100 was offered as the first prize, but this was not his incentive. It was a conscious career move. The radical and proactive town of Birmingham had pre-empted both the subsequent passion for civic pride between towns and the Municipal Corporations Act of 1835. Briggs termed it the 'civic gospel'.[6]

The winning of a major competition was one of the best ways for an architect to climb the professional ladder. Hansom was right in working to the as yet unpublished dictum 'Win a Competition and You're Made'.[7] He was right in thinking that Birmingham Town Hall would indeed 'make his name'. What he did not foresee was that the appendage 'bankrupt' gave it a sense of drama and perversely added a kind of glory. It was a life-changing experience, obliging him to leave Birmingham and at the same time bringing

---

2 *The Builder,* 8 July 1882, p.43.
3 These were St Walburge in Preston, St François-de-Sales in Boulogne, St Aloysius in Oxford and finally the church of Our Lady and St Philip Neri, later to become Arundel Cathedral.
4 One of Parliament's measures to calm unrest across the country had been the granting of a million pounds in order to build churches – 1818: 58 Geo. c. 45, Church Building Act. Those built by Oates were amongst the earliest.
5 Evinson, 'Hansom', p.317.
6 Briggs, Asa, *Victorian Cities,* London, 1996.
7 Lane, John Armstrong, *RIBAJ,* 'Win a competition and you're made', December 1865.

his association with Owen to an abrupt end. He had been exploited by the Street Commissioners who contrived to place him in the position of financial guarantor as well as architect, an unheard of and highly irregular situation. He failed to complete the project on time and ran over budget, exacerbated by a failed mason's contract on Anglesey, together with simultaneous rent due dates of the brick-yard, the wharf and the house in which he was living. Acknowledged later in life as one of his best works, the complex scenario which led to his bankruptcy brought severe, albeit temporary, personal hardship, when it first opened. It was so extreme that he said:

> My household goods were gone – my children and wife have no home to call their own – no bed to lie on – no privilege of even a house to shelter them. My aged parents are beside me, and claim my protection and support.[8]

Hansom's father, previously a superintendent of several of his son's works, was now without an income and obliged to turn to the bench, as a carpenter at the Town Hall. He was employed for one month and then discharged, by way of revenge as Hansom saw it. He bemoaned that 'bread was denied him and he had none to supply him with!' The Commissioners made use of the free services of the Liverpool architect, John Foster, to finish off what Hansom described as 'barely work left for a Clerk of Works'. Despite this when it was first opened the Town Hall was attributed to Hansom by both *The Times* and the *Birmingham Journal*. At an earlier stage, the *Birmingham Journal* had described the 'colossal magnificence and splendour of the immense room [auditorium]' in detail.[9]

However, there were mitigating circumstances, for it was here that Hansom had succumbed to Owen's influence and became radicalised. Robert Owen's charismatic personality enabled him to gather numerous devoted followers. Hansom was one such. Still comparatively young, and unavoidably embroiled with the turmoil of local politics, he relied heavily on funding for the Town Hall from the banker Thomas Attwood, the initiator of the Great Reform Bill and one of Birmingham's first Members of Parliament. When he needed money to prop up the funding of the Town Hall, the Indenture drawn up on the Isle of Anglesey, where he was building Victoria Terrace, cited the names of three members of the Attwood family, alongside two members of the Spooner family, joint owners of what was to become the largest private bank in Birmingham, located in New Street.[10] By 1801 Attwood, Spooner and Company had already established a branch in London. Both Attwood and Spooner were influential long-standing members of the Birmingham community, with Attwood having

---

8 Hansom, 'A Statement of Facts relative to the Birmingham Town-Hall, and an Appeal to the Rate-Payers and Inhabitants of Birmingham' (Birmingham, 1834), p.15.
9 *BJ*, 19 January 1833.
10 Victoria Terrace was the magnificent centrepiece of the Beaumaris regeneration plan.

been High Bailiff since 1811. Spooner was a member of the original Committee set up to consider the building of a town hall.

Battling against sixty-eight other competitors was only the first stage of a long, hard struggle. The original design had to be modified to cram into the tight site finally allocated, and then references had to be sought from two established architects. Working from fragmentary records is a necessary hazard for any historian. Correspondence is frequently one-sided; newspaper reports may or may not be accurate, and are inevitably biassed by the opinions of the editor. In this case, whilst the minutes of the Street Commissioners are extant, the loss to a fire of the minutes of the Town Hall Committee is especially frustrating, as is the loss of the official records of the Birmingham Political Union. What is clear from the evidence is that Hansom's involvement with Owen was intense, albeit brief. Following the loss of what he called 'the object of [*his*] ambition', Hansom produced a pamphlet outlining his very personal account of the events which transpired. Two of the fifteen pages of his Statement were devoted to his political thoughts.[11] In Birmingham he combined with his partner and Owen to produce a notice announcing a grand meeting to unite working builders of Great Britain and Ireland, and when strikes broke out in Derby he was so committed to the socialist cause that he was prepared to leave Birmingham in order to assist with the problems.

BIRMINGHAM TOWN HALL 1832-1834

The reasoning behind the building of the Town Hall was twofold. Not only did the growing population bring a need for larger and improved facilities for local administration, but there was also a need for a larger and better venue for the Triennial Musical Festivals, which had been held since 1778. At one stage they took place in St Philip's Church, described by the *Birmingham Argus* 'as inconvenient and as ill-suited a place for such a purpose as it is possible to conceive'.[12] No-one disagreed that it was unsuitable and anyway far too small. The local hospital, a charitable institution, was heavily dependent on the funds the festivals raised. Joseph Moore, head of the organising committee, repeatedly lobbied for a Town Hall in the 1820s, and in 1827 a petition was presented to the Street Commissioners. It was signed by 1,100 rate-payers, including Attwood.[13] However, before the Hall could be built, another Act of Parliament was necessary, in this case to agree to the raising of the rates to assist with building costs.[14]

---

11 'Statement', pp.12-13.
12 *Birmingham Argus,* November 1829.
13 *Birmingham Journal,* 8 March 1828.
14 Local and Personal Act, 9 George IV c. liv, HL/PO/PB/1/1828/9G4n91: *An Act for better paving, lighting, watching, cleansing, and otherwise improving the Town of Birmingham in the County of Warwick, and for regulation of the Police and Markets of the said Town.*

The Town Hall was not entirely altruistic. A national trend towards civic pride between towns was just beginning to emerge, and the hall was also intended as a monument to celebrate the Commissioners' achievements. When the Act was passed, it allocated £45,300 to Birmingham, of which £25,000 was set aside specifically for the purchase of land and a town hall to accommodate 3,000 people.[15] Permission was given to demolish existing buildings if necessary. Additional funds came from loans of a thousand pounds each, made by eleven citizens. This was indicative of a new up-coming middle-class involvement. The Act specified that sole use of the Hall would be given to the Governors of the Festival six weeks before, during and seven days after the event. There were already several creditable buildings in Birmingham, but as yet the town had no central focal point, nor did it have any meaningful cultural activities. Moore was so determined that 'his' concert hall would bring the prestige he sought, that he scoured the country, and also the continent, to assess similar concert halls.[16] His aim was to emulate Exeter Hall in the Strand, which had just been completed. In fact it was a close second, and stood 10 feet higher from floor to roof than the Opera House. Moore's efforts bore fruit because the Hall quickly developed a national and international reputation, especially when it hosted the first performance of Mendelssohn's *Elijah*. Takings from this amounted to £11,613, with a profit of £4,503 for the Hospital.[17] In addition to musical events, it claimed recognition as a high-profile social 'place to be seen', staging elaborate balls and many important political gatherings.

As a town, Birmingham was at the forefront of social unrest, a natural breeding ground for political activists, encouraged by the banker Thomas Attwood who believed in monetary reform and the coming together of masters and men, a theme frequently revisited by Attwood, Owen and Hansom.[18] The first brick of the Town Hall coincided with Attwood's famous New-Hall Hill Meetings in the lead-up to the passing of the Great Reform Bill.[19] Rallies had been held on New-Hall Hill since 1819, with speeches lasting for six hours.[20] These were reinstigated in 1832, leading to the notorious

---

15 See Minutes of the Street Commissioners relating to the building of the Birmingham Town Hall, 1834, 'Power to erect a Town Hall', 3-5 December 1827, Birmingham City Archives; clause xciv, 5 December 1827 refers to the purpose as being public meetings, and also a 'Music Festival for the benefit of the Birmingham General Hospital'.
16 Dent, Robert K., *The Making of Birmingham, a history of the town and its people,* (Birmingham, 1880), vol.2, p.394.
17 Dent, *Making of Birmingham,* p.395.
18 Dent, *ibid.,* p.377; Briggs, Asa, *Victorian Cities,* (London, 1996), p.143; Briggs, Asa, 'Thomas Attwood and the Economic Background of the Birmingham Political Union', *Cambridge Historical Journal,* vol.9, (1949).
19 *Birmingham Journal,* 18 May 1833.
20 Barnsby, George, J., *Birmingham Working People – A History of the Labour Movement in Birmingham 1650-1914* (Wolverhampton, 1989), p.50.

meeting of 7 May. Reports of the number of attendees vary between 80,000 and 200,000, but by any standards the meeting was vast. Attwood sought support from Hansom, asking him to address some of the rallies, and trying to persuade him to get his workmen to join in. He was apparently popular due to his 'homely language' which had particular mass appeal.[21] Delegates were called from afar, including Derby, where Hansom was later called to assist with strikes during the infamous 'Derby Lockout', as depicted later in this chapter. Attwood's main aim for this meeting was to gain support for fifty new peers prepared to accept electoral reform. When writing from London to promote this, he said 'come with hearts of lions, but with the peacefulness of lambs ... give proof that you know your rights ... you are determined to defend them'. Again he stressed 'no violence, no outrage, no disobedience ... peace, law, order, loyalty and union, those are your mottoes ... with these weapons we have gathered up our giant strength, recognised the liberty of our country, and will recover the prosperity of the people'.[22] Owen and Hansom also disapproved of violence. None of them wanted a repeat of Peterloo, and Attwood stated that he would 'not wade to reform through blood and tears'.[23] Demonstrations were organised on a festive basis, with banners naming the areas represented, along with much music. The Birmingham Political Union Hymn was encouraged at many political gatherings:

> God is our guide! No sword we draw,
> We kindle not war's battle fires;
> By Union, Justice, Reason, Law,
> We claim the birthright of our sires –
> We raise the watchword – Liberty,
> We will, we will, we will be free![24]

This pageantry was part of their appeal and, indeed, contributed to their popularity and their success. Briggs was so impressed with the way Birmingham campaigned for reform that he quotes: 'the country owed Reform to Birmingham, and its salvation from revolution'.[25]

---

21 Gillow, Joseph, *Bibliographical Dictionary of the English Catholics,* vol.3, (1995).
22 Barnsby, *Working People,* p.51.
23 Flick, Carlos, *The Birmingham Political Union and the Movements for Reform in Britain, 1830-1839* (Hamden and Folkestone, 1978), p.25; the Peterloo Massacre in Manchester had taken place in 1819 – crowds attending a peaceful demonstration were charged by the cavalry and many, including women and children, were killed.
24 Final verse of Union Hymn, Reekes, Andrew, *Speeches that changed Britain: Oratory in Birmingham* (Alcester, 205), p.16.
25 *Personal Life of George Grote* in 'Thomas Attwood and the economic background of the Birmingham Political Union', *Cambridge Historical Journal* vol.9, no.2 (London, 1948).

The Competition

Progress on the Town Hall was labouriously slow, or 'a snail's gallop' as the *Monthly Argus and Public Concensor* put it.[26] A lengthy discussion as to choice of site preceded the convoluted and protracted competition for the Town Hall, with Hansom first shortlisted and finally declared the winner.[27] Hansom and Welch submitted separate designs. Hansom's was based on the Greek temple of Castor and Pollux, a design which not only won him the competition, but also attracted nationwide publicity.[28] It was unusual in that rather than simply resembling the temple, he attempted to replicate it, using dimensions which were almost exactly three-quarters the original size.[29] Authenticity was enhanced by the use of white marble (limestone) donated by Sir Richard Bulkeley, owner of the Penmon quarries on Anglesey.[30] Hansom built The Bulkeley Arms Hotel and a Trainers House for Bulkeley, who hoped that his donation would encourage fresh contracts for his stone. Hansom's choice of style was expressly to appeal to the Commissioners by producing a building of iconic importance. The impact of the building was enhanced by being set on a podium in an island site, graphically described by Joe Holyoake as 'an ocean liner anchored in a fishing village'.[31] Due to its position, Hansom suggested that the western side should also be encased in stone.[32] The Commissioners agreed to the additional work, but refused to pay the cost, due to 'pecuniary inability'.[33]

To convince them of the validity of their low estimate, the architects and builders were obliged to agree to stand as financial guarantors, necessitating a bank loan.[34] This set an unpopular and totally unorthodox precedent. As the project progressed, Hansom spent much time trying to source materials and make economies, even to the extent that he purchased a brickyard at Selly Oak and personally bargained for timber. When preparing the foundations,

---

26 *Monthly Argus and Public Concensor,* October 1830.
27 Hansom, 'Statement', p.5.
28 The design was taken from Taylor and Cresy's *Architectural Antiquities of Rome*, see Frank Salmon, 'Storming the Campo Vaccino': British Architects and the Antique Buildings of Rome after Waterloo; *Architectural History*, 38 (1995).
29 Henry-Russell Hitchcock, *Early Victorian Architecture in Britain* (London, 1973), pp.299, 300; Salmon, 'Campo Vaccino', p.164, n.84.
30 Dent, *The Making of Birmingham: being a history of the rise and growth of the Midland metropolis* (London, 1894), p.376; contract between William Thomas and others (builders) and William Hughes and others (stonemasons) for providing and working blocks of Anglesey White Marble for the Birmingham Town Hall, Anglesey Record Office, WM/322/2; for a full description of merits and workability of Anglesey limestone, see Philip Brannon, 'A Visit to the Marble Quarries of Anglesea', *North Wales Chronicle,* 17 March 1877.
31 Holyoak, Joe, *All About Victoria Square,* Birmingham (1989), p.7.
32 Hansom, 'Statement', p.8; Cunningham, Colin, *Victorian and Edwardian Town Halls*, (London, 1981), p.175.
33 Hansom, 'Statement', p.8.
34 Dent, *Making of Birmingham*, p.377; Assignment of monies borrowed in connection with the building of Birmingham Town Hall, 23 August 1833, *AA*, WM/322/3.

he had already made use of the hard clay layer which was above the lower level of rock, turning it into some two hundred thousand bricks. These had the convenience of being made, dried and burnt on site, with a special kiln set up for the purpose. He was given free tonnage by the late Captain Bradshaw for stone along the Duke of Bridgewater's canal, but lost 'at least £200 in actual money' when the stonemason let him down in Anglesey.[35]

From the time of the announcement of the competition, if not before, dramatic events occurred in rapid succession. 1833 was particularly fraught, with several distractions which contributed to Hansom's bankruptcy. Firstly there was a tragic accident in February, when a hook on a pulley-block gave way and three of his workmen fell from a height of 70 foot. Hansom had introduced 'a new species of machinery to raise the framed tie beams and principals to the top of the building'.[36] No-one was held to blame for the accident, but two of the men died.[37] The building trade in general was overshadowed by widespread strikes and the setting up of unions. Hansom and Welch were as intent on resolving these as much as they were on completing their cherished Town Hall. Hansom met delegates from Manchester and Liverpool in Birmingham, on their return home from a protest in London. Postgate wrote that when there were arguments between any of the trades, it was usually between London and Manchester, 'with Birmingham the battleground'.[38] He wrote to Owen accordingly:

> There are 800 men, at a rough guess, concerned in the Manchester strike – we calculate that 10/- per week per head would maintain them in work if a provision store be established, from whence rations could be distributed to them for labour notes. If they make their own bricks – and could arrange with the Colliers' Union for coals to burn them with – little if any more of cash would be wanted than the £400 per week – and in one month so much of capital would be accumulated as would be worth at least 8 times the sum. Some idea of this is now sown in the minds of 8 confederates of this morning, and from the avidity with which they received the principle I expect it to shoot out a wonderful tree in a few hours.[39]

Notice, September 1833

Things reached a stage when Hansom and Welch were so heavily involved that they almost acted as business managers for Owen. Owen latched onto

---

35 'Statement', p.8.
36 Dent, *Making of Birmingham*, p.376.
37 Their memorial in St Philip's Churchyard, is commemorated annually by the National Workers Union to honour people who have been killed in workplace accidents.
38 Postgate, *Builders' History* (London, 1923), p.85.
39 Letter Hansom to Owen, 18 August 1833, R.O. 651.

Hansom and Welch, not the other way round, for, as Postgate put it, they were 'completely trusted and followed'.[40] Further, Welch was beginning to pick up Owen's rhetoric. The Operative Builders' Union, a federation of seven trades in the building industry, was described as 'a new life and a new light' and Welch said they were 'planting a giant Tree the top whereof shall reach to Heaven and afford shelter to all succeeding generations'.[41] Hansom and Welch then drew up a manifesto announcing a meeting which drew attention to the plight of builders and how their work had been impacted by the introduction of machinery. The manifesto called for the formation of a GRAND NATIONAL GUILD of BUILDERS, listing numerous professions from architect to bricklayer, set out in a similar way to that which Hansom quoted when he set up his subsequent *Builder* journal. The Union was to safeguard jobs and pay, provide education for adults and children alike, and generally ensure humanitarian conditions analogous to those which Owen had provided in New Lanark. It also stressed that operations were to be in 'harmony'.

Birmingham Grammar School, September 1833

With the Town Hall well underway, the Street Commissioners proposed a further development, the replacement of King Edward's School, or the 'free Grammer Schole' [*sic*]. This was quite a bold move as the school had been founded in 1552, but they had little choice as it was falling into a state of decay and some of the walls were crumbling.[42] The job was not given to Hansom. It was inevitable that he would lose the competition, if for no reason other than that architects were required to provide securities amounting to two-thirds of the contract. He was not, of course, in a position to do that. Hansom was somewhat aggrieved, assuming that, as architect of the Town Hall, he would automatically be appointed for the Grammar School. His sympathies towards Owen had engendered a measure of ill-feeling and may have been held against him, but by then his sobriquet as the 'The Socialist Architect' was well entrenched. Welch expressed their joint views in a letter to an architect colleague in Leeds, saying:

> My partner and myself with his [Owen's] assistance are endeavouring so to organise the great working mass of builders in the kingdom as to place them in a permanent position of comfort and happiness – and to destroy that ruinous system of competition amongst their guilds which has reduced them to misery and involved us in almost incessant anxiety and care.[43]

---

40 Postgate, *ibid.,* p.90.
41 Postgate, *Builders' History,* p.84 citing the above.
42 Dent, *Making of Birmingham,* vol.3, p.444.
43 Letter Welch to Chantrel esqre., 12 September 1833, R.O. 662.

Hansom had previously written to Owen stating that he had 'drilled' the carpenters into 'condition', and would do so with the plasterers and similarly with the masons.[44]

Meanwhile, Hansom prepared to go ahead with work on the school, convinced that 'The Governors cannot carry on the work without us ... either [they] must come to terms with the unionists or work would stop'. He suggested that this would be an ideal opportunity for brick-makers to start making their own bricks, with rations provided in the form of labour notes. Manchester strikers were hesitant to take part, and when Hansom suggested that Owenites could provide the necessary securities, they failed to respond. The outcome was out of his control. He described the builder's conduct as 'indefensible', but Messrs Walthew, the most influential (and wealthy) building firm in Birmingham took over, dismissing all workers who were members of Unions.[45] The corollary to this was that Hansom's financial difficulties put a block on his entering the competition for the building of the new Houses of Parliament, which was awarded to Charles Barry, the appointed architect for the school.

Perhaps it was as well that they were not winners for their workload was already over-stretched. Nevertheless they were strong contenders. A lengthy editorial in the *Birmingham Journal* displays a picture of their design, along with a strong preference in its favour and outspoken criticism of (Sir) Charles Barry's winning entry. The editorial complained that Barry's design was clever, incorporating textbook examples of Gothic architecture, but totally lacking in any originality or sense of adventure, likening it to a 'pile of Manchester houses ... a gingerbread of a thing', which, instead of enhancing New-street, debased it. But then, if convenience of design was the only criterion, why the exorbitant cost? In a hyperthetical argument the editor continued to mock the choice of the 'Gothic hobby', stating that a utilitarian building could have been erected for £5,000, not the £40,000 which was proposed. The argument bounced to and fro. When Gothic was said to give an 'historical' effect to the building, a sarcastic response was given. Finally the writer asked 'the good people of Birmingham' if 'we cannot do what we like with our own?' The article continued in considerable detail, pulling apart every aspect of the design and layout, complaining about such things as unnecessarily lengthy passages, dungeon-like staircases and the master's room being so close to the street that he might be a shopkeeper in need of a place to display his wares! The ultimate insult refers to the 'abomination of the square courts', enclosed by high buildings and only of use to astronomers.

It was at this stage that Hansom's partner, Edward Welch stepped in, writing to inform Owen of the situation and enclosing a copy of the ultimatum

---

44 Letter Hansom to Owen, 6 September 1833, R.O. 657.
45 Letter Hansom to Owen, 12 September 1833, R.O. 656.

and manifesto which he and Hansom had drawn up and which they hoped would be adopted by several lodges of the Building Trade. The manifesto was also sent to Mr Walthew direct in an attempt to bring work to a halt.[46] It was defiant in tone, stating that 'We the delegates of the several lodges of the Building Trades ... elected for correcting abuses ... do give notice that you will receive no assistance from the working men in any of our bodies to enable you to fulfill an engagement with the Governors of the Free Grammar School ... you had no authority from us to make such an engagement ...'.

Apart from the problems with the Grammar School, Hansom personally suffered strikes at the Town Hall when he was criticised by the very people for whom he was trying to make improvements. Some of his own men complained that they were not receiving a fair wage. It appeared that Joseph's 'cavalcade' extended beyond his immediate family and included a considerable part of his workforce. He justified his rates of pay in Birmingham by pointing out that he paid a flat rate wherever they were working, so that whilst it might appear that he was paying less than the going rate in Birmingham, in other areas he had paid well above local wages.

Operative Builders' Guildhall, November 1833

At the week-long 'Builders' Parliament' held in Manchester in September 1833, it was decreed that the Operative Builders should become a Guild for Co-operative self-employment. The meeting was dominated by Owen, Hansom and Welch.[47] With a new guild in mind, and still struggling to finance the Town Hall, Hansom gave his own time and his own money to the building of an Operative Builders' Guildhall. The estimated cost was £2,000. News spread to Leicester, where it was reported that the procession which accompanied the laying of the foundation stone was one of an entirely new and important character ... being a congregation of the united trades.[48] Beneath the stone Hansom placed a box containing a parchment which said that the work was being commenced 'in the confident hope of a new era in the condition of the whole of the working classes of the world'.[49] He used an Owenite-type principle, whereby relays of unemployed building artificers worked for two or three days a week each and were paid by contributions of others from ten different branches of the building trade who were in full employment. On a number of occasions, as exemplified by the report on the Grammar School, the *Birmingham Journal* described his work favourably, and in detail. It also showed how Hansom had adapted Owen's ideas to suit the building trade:

---
46 Letter Welch to Owen, 6 September 1833, R.O. 657.
47 Postgate, *Builders' History,* p.94.
48 *Leicester Chronicle,* 7 December 1833.
49 Postgate, *Builders' History,* p.101.

> We hear that different tradesmen approving of the exemplary behaviour of the workmen engaged in this undertaking, have promised them assistance, especially in hardware, and glass, and lead. Great labour is intended to be bestowed on various parts of the building, the workmen availing themselves of the long winter nights to prepare the ornamental work. The front will be a mixture of stone and brickwork, and the interior of the large room will be elaborately enriched by the plasterer's art … this sort of extra labour is to be gratuitous and voluntary, and intended to serve as a specimen of the skill and taste of the projectors. The least … of ornaments, aided by the painter's talent, is calculated to be eminently beautiful. In the centre will be a figure of Peace. We should observe, that the great room, is on the first floor and is 78 feet long by 30 feet wide and 24 feet high. On the ground level are several smaller rooms for committees, and cellars in the basement. … this edifice is for the Guild or Brotherhood of Operative Builders, in which it is their intention, besides holding their meetings for general business, to have schools for children by day, and in the evening for adults; the course of education for the latter will be the useful and scientific branches of their profession, illustrated by models and drawings, and further enforced by the delivery of lectures.[50]

Hansom asked Owen for £500 in order to complete the project.[51] His response is unknown, but it is unlikely that he was in a position to oblige. However, whilst in Anglesey, the financial burden of the Town Hall was placed on Welch, who seized the title deeds of the Guildhall as security for materials. It was months before work could proceed. Hansom was also concerned as to the length of time he was away from Birmingham. He seemed to rate his own contribution very highly. Writing to Owen he said that he had been for the last six weeks in Anglesey forwarding the Masons' work at the Quarries, and 'it is likely that unless I take some proper step now, I shall be punished and justly for my subservience … for my apparent abandonment of the Trades [Union] when my presence was almost as necessary to them as the keystone to the Arch'.[52] Further, he added, 'it is of vital importance to the question of *Independence of Labour* and to the regeneration of the country that this project of building the Guildhall should not be defeated'. This was no exaggeration. The Union had no structural base, no visible 'home', for there was nothing in London or anywhere else. It was abandoned in June 1834 and work was taken over by the landlord. The building in Broad Street [sometimes erroneously described as Shadwell Street] was never used as a Guildhall, but ignominiously became a

---

50 *BJ*, 21 December 1833.
51 Letter Hansom to Owen, 23 February 1834, R.O. 676.
52 *Ibid*.

metal warehouse.[53] Had it been completed and fully functioning, it would have provided a central core, a focus for future activities, and the Union might well have lasted much longer.

Derby, December 1833 – early 1834
The year ended with yet another 'absence without leave'. Welch chose this moment to get married, and from then onwards Hansom was Owen's sole intermediary where strikes were concerned. He duly went to Derby where the major strike which led to the notorious Turnout (or lock-out) was brewing. News of the BPU fuelled existing discontent, mainly due to low wages. Like Owen, they believed that:

> everything which was produced belonged to those who by their labour produced it and ought to be shared among them, that there ought to be no accumulation of capital in the hands of anyone to enable him to employ others as labour, and thus by becoming a master make them slaves under the name of workmen.[54]

Derby organised a petition which was sent to the Prime Minister, the Duke of Wellington, stating that something should be done to relieve the plight of the poor. Crowds gathered in the town and, as at Peterloo, peaceful protests erupted into violence. Totally independent of Birmingham, the Derby Political Union was then formed.

Along with Attwood and many others, Derby was disappointed at the outcome of the Great Reform Bill, which only provided a marginal increase of voting rights – hardly universal suffrage. The Turnout which transpired was triggered by a single workman refusing to pay a fine for alleged poor workmanship. Eight hundred men 'came out' in his support, and this rose to thirteen hundred, a third of the population. Within three months it had risen to two thousand. They survived on 7s. per week. Owen's Derby agent for *The Pioneer* called for collections to support the strikers. Donations were sent from fifteen areas, including £20 from Birmingham and £20 from Hansom's future home town, Hinckley. The Birmingham Labour movement set up a special 'Derby Committee' and sent supplies in the form of bacon, whilst Pare urged Birmingham trade unionists to plan provision stores.[55] A message from the General National Collective Trades Unions (GNCTU), optimistically declared 'Men of Derby, fear not; your cause is won'. The Derby workers even considered purchasing their own mill. The committee (or possibly

---
53 RIBA archives, Professor Stephen Welsh, correspondence file, WeS.
54 Pike, E. Royston (ed.), *Human documents of the Industrial Revolution* (London, 1966) p.132, quoted by Stevenson, Graham, *Defence or Defiance? Derbyshire and the fight for democracy*, (Croydon, 2014).
55 Garnett, *Co-operation*, p.141

Hansom) estimated that it would cost £1,680 to build, with £1,221 required for machinery. This was out of their reach, and would only have employed ten per cent of the unemployed workers. The employers took charge. They produced a 'Document' which workers had to sign, declaring that they were not union members. Anyone who refused to sign was refused employment. The employers by-passed new child labour laws and took on 'black sheep' from other towns, and even from abroad.[56] As a deterrent, names of the so-called 'black sheep', were published in *The Pioneer.*

It is not clear precisely what part Hansom played in all this, but his involvement is mentioned in his obituary. As for Owen, he seemed to have his head in the clouds. He spoke to the employers and the workmen separately. His philosophising, his pacifist stance and his ideas on class reconciliation lost him credibility. He offered to return as a mediator when what was most needed was hard cash. Owen was following his own agenda and the workers in Derby felt let down by both Owen and the GNCTU. The Grand Union was never fully operational and floundered after its leader, James Morrison, left in March 1834. Owen closed both *The Pioneer* and *The Crisis,* which he felt were exacerbating the situation, and from then onwards contributions began to dwindle noticeably. A sum of £230 was sent to Derby by the builders in April, but this was not enough.[57] The burden upon the strikers was untenable and though they still supported unions in principle, most returned to work. Small groups such as the Derby Carpenters and Joiners Society re-grouped. It is possible that Hansom had initiated the builder's contribution, but as he was by then also lacking an income, he could do no more.

MOVE TO HINCKLEY

Disillusioned, he pulled back from politics and resumed a more conventional, if less dramatic, career. This meant relinquishing the house he was building for himself in George Street near Newhall Hill and moving to another area. Before re-inventing himself as 'the Catholic architect', Hansom was commissioned to design a bank in Hinckley, Leicestershire. His employer was Dempster Hemming, Attwood's preferred parliamentary candidate for North Warwickshire.[58] The following year Hemming invited him to move to his estate at Caldecote on the Warwickshire/Leicestershire border. Despite having been bankrupted, his management skills were acknowledged. He had after all been directing his master mason and a workforce of over two hundred men, ordering supplies and chasing funds, in addition to ensuring the satisfactory completion of the building. In his new post, he acted as banker, ran a coal-mining business

---

56 Owen particularly objected to child labour. In the Darley Mills they started work at 4 o'clock in the morning and finished at 8 o'clock. For this they were paid 15d. a week.
57 *The Crisis,* 12 April 1834 and 29 April 1834.
58 Moss, David, J., *Thomas Attwood, the Biography of a Radical,* (Canada, 1990), p.237.

and generally managed the estate, a position not so far removed from Owen's at New Lanark.[59] Enabled by the Country Banking Act, Hansom then went on to build a second bank, near Caldecote, and finally built the Hinckley Union Workhouse, resulting from the Poor Law Amendment Act of 1834. Thus, he was so well-informed as to current affairs that he was able to distance himself from Owen and operate in his professional capacity at the forefront of change. However his intended design for the new Metropolitan Music Hall pre-empted future use of iron in buildings. Described as 'Hansom's New System of Building', it was too advanced and never came to fruition.[60]

The Builder 1842

During his short spell in Hinckley, where he lived above one of his banks, Hansom took time to establish a journal, *The Builder*, for he considered that his burgeoning profession was 'in sad want of some channel of intercommunication and illustration' and needed a public voice. Brooks believed that this project originated from his time in Birmingham, but it was given final impetus by the newly formed *Illustrated London News,* which was launched shortly before *The Builder*.[61] Owen, too could have had some influence, for he was constantly producing newspapers and pamphlets which he either wrote, edited or to which he contributed. In Hansom's precursor, or preliminary issue of *The Builder*, he said he was aiming to address the interests of the whole Building Business, from Builder to Labourer, conjoining the characteristics of a Trade Journal, Magazine and Newspaper. The inclusion of illustrations and diagrams was significant. Not only were they most informative, but up until this time printing facilities had only been able to produce text. There was no official training for architects and the few books which were available were very expensive, an added reason why he produced his journal. Wishing to be all-inclusive, the full title of the journal was *The Builder: A Journal for the Architect, Engineer, Operative and Artist.* Some architects queried his choice of wording, but he insisted that it should be for 'all classes (an Owenism), and crafts concerned in the art of building itself and the art with which it is allied'.[62] The 1851 census identified a total of 60,000 builders, the second largest occupational group in the country, with an annual turnover of millions.[63] This should have given his journal a very considerable circulation.

Hansom's pre-cursor was used to test the market. A list of eighty possible disciplines or topics was given, but due to financial constraints he didn't

---

59 *The Builder,* July 1882, p.44.
60 *The Architect's Magazine,* 2 April 1842.
61 Brooks, Michael, 'The Builder' in the 1840s: The Making of a Magazine, the Shaping of a Profession', *Victorian Periodicals Review,* 14, no.3 (Fall, 1981).
62 Pre-cursor, p.8.
63 Himmelfarb, Gertrude, 'The Culture of Poverty', in H. J. Dyos and Michael Wolff (eds), *The Victorian City: The Novel between City and Country* (London, 1973), p.710.

remain editor long enough to achieve all he had hoped, including a register of vacancies. Amongst the topics he did include were some of a technical nature, some of academic antiquarian interest and a variety of general topics, so as to interest the wider public. The pre-cursor contained many advertisements and gave much publicity to the works and writings of his colleague, John Claudius Loudon, the Scottish botanist and landscaper from Birmingham who was responsible for designing the Birmingham Botanical Gardens in 1832. Hansom tried to remain apolitical, but some social or quasi-political issues were raised. Evinson interpreted an editorial in Hansom's final issue of *The Builder* as a 'plea for resuscitation of Trade Guilds'.[64] Hansom wrote:

> if we had been disposed, we frankly own in the face of the world, that our first choice would be the workmen ... when we consider that there are some five hundred thousand working builders in this United Empire ... we can never lose sight of the fact ... that if there be anything for which this paper [*The Builder*] may find it worth while to live, it must be through, dependent on, and working for this mass of industry.

He went on to say that 'for ten years we urged and insisted on the necessity of trade incorporation ... if before ten years elapse, we have not our local and grand incorporation of the trade, then we will venture to say we shall have their discorporation and destruction'. Hansom believed that an added bonus to incorporation would be an end to strikes and violence, and regulation of wages. Owen's influence continues to shine through as he mentions the setting up of [art] schools and 'brotherhood for the suffering and unfortunate'. The new Act, which replaced a previous version, included minute regulations prescribing the required solidity of foundations, thickness of walls and scantlings of floor and roof timbers, as well as for all apartments to have a fireplace and a window to secure a ventilation current. This came into force in January 1845. Incorporation never took place. Alfred Bartholomew, Hansom's immediate successor, published a supplement to issue number 9 entitled the 'Cyclopaedia of the New Metropolitan Building Act' and printed the act in full in issue number 12.

Hansom also campaigned for improved housing and the preservation of health. An early environmentalist, he included a report on smoke nuisance and the effect of toxic chemicals in his journal. Like Bartholomew (who suffered an early death), George Godwin, the next editor, also shared his social stance, and Hansom continued to contribute whenever he felt the need arose. Though not published until 1842, the article, headed 'Treatment of Work-People by their Employers' demonstrates that Owen's principles were

---

64 Evinson, 'Hansom', p.145.

being acted upon at a national level. It refers to progress being made through means of a parliamentary inquiry into payment of wages:

> it had been shewn that there are persons extensively engaged in manufactures of various kinds, who feel that the employment of bodies of workpeople involves a degree of responsibility to care for their general well-being, and who act on that conviction in a manner highly creditable to themselves, and conducive to the excellent object they have in view. These employers are of [the] opinion that to regard as a machine a man whose skill or industry assists them to maintain their own families in respectability, is altogether unchristian, and that by viewing work-people in such light, they would deprive themselves of some of the finest opportunities of usefulness, and of cementing the bonds of society.[65]

The article goes on to cite examples of deductions made to assist with medical care and education, one being that 'each child is expected to pay one penny a week'.

Colleges 1842

The most important feature of his journal was the announcement of his Builders College. On three separate occasions, Hansom attempted to set up a college, the first and most important one of which was advertised prominently in his pre-cursor of *The Builder*. This ambitious undertaking also failed due to lack of capital, a back-lash from Birmingham. The other two attempts were on a smaller scale, the second whilst he was living in Preston and the third, an ecclesiastical art school, started in Leith, near Edinburgh. This had to close when a local Bishop withdrew his funding.

The advertisement for the 'Builders College' gives much detail.[66] Students were to live in the house in central London which he had acquired from the architect Charles Barry after the latter had relocated to work on the new Houses of Parliament. Applicants were not to be less than fourteen years of age and would remain in residence until they were 'competent to practice a liberal and lucrative profession'. Hansom's college was thorough, with college discipline and systematic tuition under proficient masters, who would also oversee the 'morals, habits and health' of the students. There would be an abundant supply of books and outings to inspect buildings. A mix of school, office and workshop, he put old methods into a new format, stressing the need for an understanding of manual and craft skills as much as theoretical knowledge. Accordingly, his syllabus was very wide, ranging from design,

---

65 *The Builder,* precursor, p.4.
66 *The Builder, ibid.,* p.6.

draughtsmanship and mechanics to book-keeping, and from philosophy and general literature to languages. French, German and Italian were considered essential for trips abroad. Hansom acknowledged that it was a 'giant work', but he anticipated a growing need for well-trained architects. At this time, anyone could describe themself as an 'architect' and the profession did not have a good reputation, mainly due to over-charging. Even after the Institute of British Architects was formed in 1837 (subsequently the Royal Institute of British Architects), there was still no formal training on offer.[67] Without saying as much, Hansom is underlining Owen's theory, the importance of early upbringing, and particularly education. It is telling that both his journal and his college refer to 'building', not 'architecture'. The time for specialisation, such as architect, engineer and surveyor, had yet to come, and though Hansom saw himself as an architect, he was still locked into the past when he said 'builder'. The College provided examinations, but had it been successful, a need would have arisen for the accreditation of an official body.

Hansom had moved into a very different phase of his life and the professionalisation of architecture became paramount. There is no doubt that his extraneous political activities had been a major contributory factor leading to his temporary financial demise. Furthermore, he considered that the Street Commissioners had known from the outset that work could not be completed within the low estimate he had submitted. He was so bitter that in his Statement he described them as 'despotic'.[68] Hansom also admitted that had he not chosen to use man-power rather than machinery for the building of the town hall, he could have saved thirty per cent in overheads.[69] Nevertheless, the long-term benefits are incalculable. Furthermore, it would not be an exaggeration to say that the Town Hall reformed Birmingham as much as the Reform Bill reformed the nation, thus, to better understand the background which led to these events, the following chapter will look at Birmingham in more depth.

---

67 Membership of the RIBA was not compulsory until 1938.
68 'Statement', p.3.
69 *Ibid.*, p.13.

8. Engraving of York 1840 by W. Harvey

Hansom's work in Beaumaris:

9(a). Beaumaris gaol

9(b). Bulkeley Arms Hotel

9(c). Victoria Terrace

9(d). Trainer's (Chantry) House

10. Attwood and Spooner bank

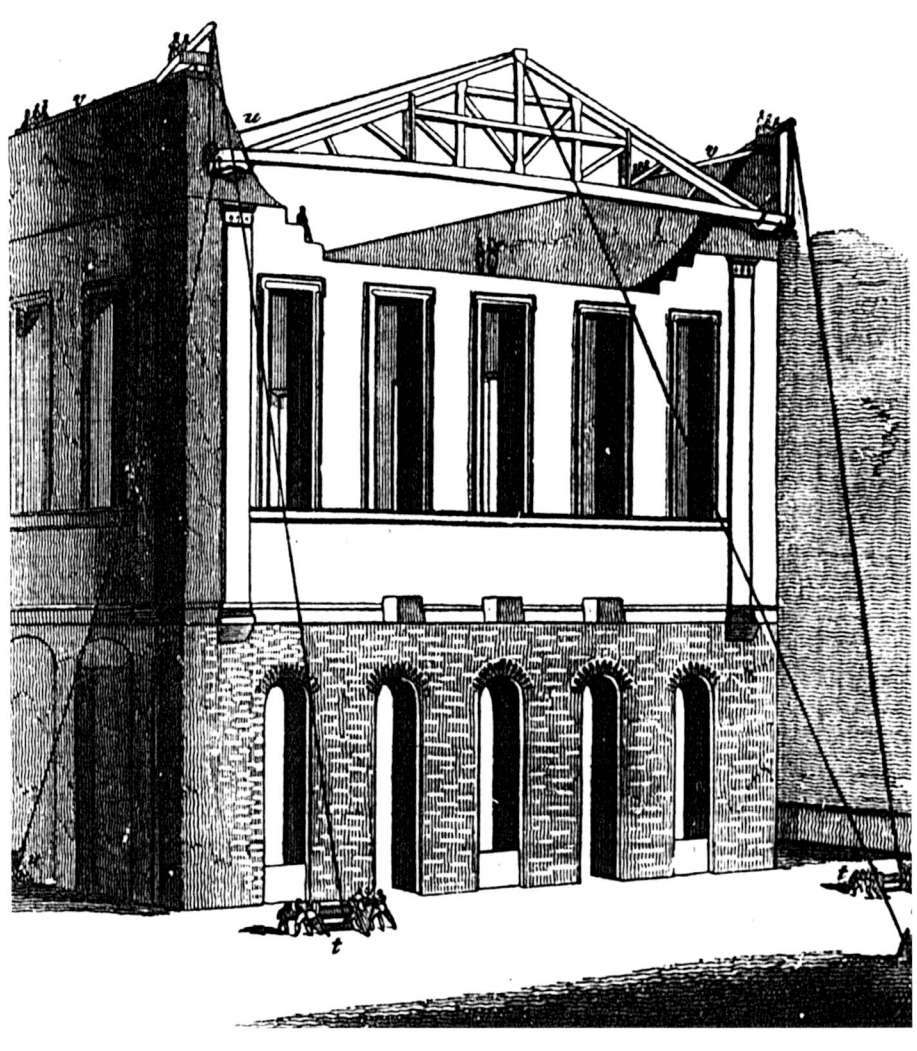

11. Raising Rafters

12. Memorial of Badger and Heap

At a GRAND MEETING of all the Members of all the Lodges of Manchester, called by special Notification to each Lodge, to meet ROBERT OWEN, JOSEPH HANSOM, and EDWARD WELCH, held in the Manor House, Brown-street, Manchester, on Thursday, 12th Sept. 1833:

ROBERT OWEN, IN THE CHAIR.

The Chairman, after stating the servile and deplorable condition to which the producers of wealth, throughout Great Britain and Ireland, have been reduced by competition with machinery and with each other, and explaining to the meeting the utter impossibility of any permanent improvement being effected for their benefit while this competition shall be permitted to be continued, submitted to them the following proposals, as a certain, speedy and effectual mode of giving a new direction to the industry of the Building classes, and as a means of placing them and their children and their children's children in a state of permanent independence.

UNION.

To the United Working Builders of Great Britain and Ireland.

Proposals for the Establishment of a National Association for Building, to be called "THE GRAND NATIONAL GUILD OF BUILDERS, to be composed of Architects, and Surveyors,—Masons,—Carpenters and Joiners, Bricklayers,—Plasterers,—Slaters,—Plumbers and Glaziers, and Painters,—Whitesmiths,—Quarrymen,—and Brickmakers.

OBJECTS OF THE UNION.

1. The general improvement of all the individuals forming the Building Class; ensuring regular employment to all.
2. To ensure fair remuneration for their services.
3. To fix a reasonable time for labour.
4. To educate both Adults and Children.
5. To have regular superior Medical Advice and assistance, and to make provision for the comfortable and independent retirement of the aged and infirm.
6. To regulate the operations of the whole in harmony, and to produce a general fund sufficient to secure all these objects.
7. To ensure a superiority of Building for the Public at fair and equitable prices.
8. To obtain good and comfortable Dwellings for every Member of the Union—extensive and well arranged Workshops,—Places of Depôt for Building Materials,—Provisions and Clothing,—Halls for the Meeting of the Lodges and Central Committees,—Schools and Academies for the instruction of Adults and Children in Morals and the useful Sciences.
9. And also the Establishment of Builders' Banks in the various districts in which the Grand District Lodges shall be established.

13. Notice of Builders' Union

14. Operative Builders' Guildhall

15. Banner regarding Derby Lockout

THE BUILDER.

BUILDERS' COLLEGE, LONDON.—To PARENTS AND GUARDIANS.—Mr. HANSOM, Architect of the Birmingham Town Hall, &c. &c., has associated with his practice an Institution to give enlarged facilities to students in Architecture and Architectural Engineering; and to form a superior class of Architectural Sculptors, Carvers, Modellers, &c., to be engaged in his own office and works until competent to practise a liberal and lucrative profession.

It has been Mr. Hansom's study to lay down a plan for the instruction of architectural decorators and furnishers, which shall combine the advantages of the school, the office, and the workshop; so that general education, professional training, and handicraft skill may be acquired and perfected together—that the benefits of college discipline, and residence of systematic tuition under proficient masters, of lectures and examinations, and of constant familiarity with books, models, and works may be united in one establishment.

Pupils are eligible at the age of fourteen and upwards, and are articled in the usual manner as apprentices. The terms are moderate, and with other particulars, may be known on application at the office, 27, Foley-place, London.

16. Notification of Builders' College

CHAPTER III

BIRKMINGHAM –

the town, the people and politics

If upbringing and environment are fundamental to the 'formation of character' for people, they are equally fundamental to the character of a town. The village of New Lanark would never have come about had it not been for its spectacular waterfall. Harmony Hall might not have been such a dismal failure had it not been that the location and the purpose to which Owen tried to put it were totally incompatible. Likewise, despite the unimaginable growth and the relentless onslaught of recent, uncompromising changes which have taken place in Birmingham, at heart Birmingham is still Birmingham. This chapter looks at the town and its main protagonists, concluding with the various convoluted political machinations taking place during this period.

EARLY YEARS
Strangely, it was a mix of its central location in England, combined with the lack of water transport which gave Birmingham much of its early character. Its origins lay in a small Anglo-Saxon village of less than 3,000 acres (the same size as Queen Wood Farm which Owen purchased for his ultimate community), with neither sea nor river, and with canals only built at the end

of the eighteenth century, and the first railway in 1837.[1] The town had no choice but to be self-dependent. Not only were other towns more readily accessible, but they were typically founded on a pyramidal social hierarchy, dominated by landed gentry and large employers. Birmingham's nearest rivals, Liverpool and Manchester took advantage of the industrial revolution, the one a busy sea port and the other soon to be the centre of large, factory-based cotton production. Owen's background was firmly rooted in large-scale industry, cotton and textiles. On the other hand, Birmingham was already making its way in a different direction as it gained a reputation for toy-making, not children's toys as of today, but small, high-quality specialist items based on metal-work. It was noted for gun-making and its Jewellery Quarter as well as buttons, buckles and nails. These were produced in small units of only a few people, in comparatively peaceful conditions without any cut-throat rivalry. However, there was extensive migration as a decline in the country's economy led people from the country to seek work in the town. The population nearly doubled between 1800 and 1831.[2] The kaleidoscope of diverse in-comers from diverse backgrounds gave birth to the persona of the 'Brummagem'. They developed strong characteristics; they were proud, hard-working and hard-drinking, innovative and entrepreneurial, but above all independent. Hopkins succinctly described the stereotyped picture of Birmingham in terms which would have suited Owen, as 'a scene of class co-operation rather than one of class conflict'.[3] This was an ideal foundation for the events which were to occur.

Housing in Birmingham was well above many of its northern counterparts. There were some back-to-backs (now demolished), but none had cellars, and most people in the early nineteenth-century were housed in courts, with a few allotments. Underground drainage and a good supply of clean water ensured healthy conditions.[4] One official report in the 1840s stated:

> Birmingham ... a favourable contrast ... with the state of other large towns ... each family living in a separate dwelling is conducive to comfort and cleanliness, with dry and absorptive nature of the soil a very great natural advantage.[5]

though later reports suggest that there was some deterioration, perhaps due to overcrowding.

---

1 Royle, *millennium*, p.75; the first train service was from Birmingham to Derby in 1839, followed by Birmingham to London in 1842.
2 In 1800 the population was 74,000, in 1831 it had risen to 147,000, and by 1851 it was 233,000.
3 Hopkins, Eric, *Birmingham: The First Manufacturing Town in the World 1760-1840* (London, 1989), p.180.
4 Hopkins, *Birmingham*, p.5.
5 Hopkins, *ibid.*, p.122.

Working conditions and pay of highly skilled workers was sufficient for some of them to own their own houses.[6] With this in mind, it is easy to see why Hansom's builders came out on strike. He assured them that they were being paid the same rate as in Liverpool and elsewhere, but the men had some justification in claiming, 'but this is Birmingham'! Builders apart, workshops were run on an unconventional, quasi flexi-time basis – far removed from Owen's rigid working hours at New Lanark – and were paid an hourly rate. Workers were not autonomous, but they insisted upon taking holiday time, such as Whitsun and Christmas. Furthermore 'Saint Monday' was the norm, whereby, possibly suffering from hangovers, work would be slow or non-existent on Mondays, accelerating during the rest of the week in order to increase their pay.[7] Employers were entrepreneurs and inventors, yet tolerant and paternalistic towards their workforce. Typically working from the home of the master brought an atmosphere of informality and a relaxed working relationship. Thus there was a well-established ideal which was highly successful. The downside was that even they depended upon child labour.

In 1775, long before Owen moved to New Lanark, Matthew Boulton of Birmingham was unusual in that he claimed to own the largest factory in the world.[8] He was an exceptional employer, who achieved a thousand employees, and he believed that happy workers were good workers. Like many entrepreneurs at this time, he was dependent upon loans, had some good luck (two wealthy wives), and had several difficult times, which brought him close to bankruptcy. However, he built a factory at Hockley Brook, just two miles from the centre of Birmingham, where he was able to take advantage of watermills, and, like Owen, his factory became a tourist attraction. Boulton believed in mechanical devices, which were used in tandem with people, to save time and labour. This was a more sympathetic approach, unlike that in Manchester, where machines were considered to be substitutes for humans.[9] His experience, enhanced by having joined together with James Watt of steam engine fame, was unusual in Birmingham, but it shows how advanced the town was and that Owen was not the only person to develop and manage a large scale project. On-site accommodation was available on Boulton's factory site, more by way of convenience than any pretence at a community, with rent deducted from pay. The only education appeared to be a drawing school, presumably to create designs for his products. Records do not indicate working hours or child labour, but Boulton looked after his workers inasmuch as they were given annual outings, supported by a health

---

6 Hopkins, *ibid.,* p.182.
7 Kesteven, G.R., *The Triumph of Reform 1832,* (London, 1967), p.102; see also Davis, George, *Saint Monday or Scenes from Love Life* (1790).
8 Hopkins, *Birmingham,* p.86.
9 Briggs, Asa, *Victorian Cities,* p.142.

insurance scheme and, in 1799 at least, were all given Christmas presents.[10] He spent much time in London, where he had a show room, and associated with royalty, noblemen and foreign ambassadors by way of promotion for his business. (His partner complained that he was away too often!) Thus, with no pre-knowledge of Owen's philosophies, many parallels in *modus operandi* can be identified.

Critical Years

The period between 1829 (Owen's return from America) and 1834 (Hansom's bankruptcy) was as critical for the nation as it was for Birmingham, and individually for Attwood, Owen and Hansom. Events occurred in rapid succession, in several directions at once. To add to the upheavals, there were frequent changes of Prime Minister, including the appointment of the unpopular Duke of Wellington, who Attwood described as 'being unfit to govern'.[11] By the time Owen came back to England, William Pare, a tobacconist and cigar retailer in New Street, had already founded the Birmingham Co-operative Society. Though the Society had purchased a few acres on the outskirts of the town to form what he termed 'a farming community', Pare warned of the risks of relinquishing a steady income in the expectation of selling surplus produce. Firstly the surplus was not instant, and secondly capital was required to set up the arrangement.[12] Surely predictive? Simple, common sense advice which Owen, the astute and successful business-man from Lancashire and New Lanark bypassed when trying to establish Harmony Hall.

In 1831 the first attempt was made to launch Attwood's would-be Great Reform Bill, the Ralahine community was founded in Ireland, and Hansom and Welch were appointed architects for the Town Hall. By the following year National Equitable Exchanges had been set up and the foundation stone laid for the Town Hall. During this period, Attwood founded the Birmingham Political Union [of all classes], to protect rights of the public and unite the middle and working classes.[13] He orchestrated and carefully managed his massive rally at Newhall Hill, at which Daniel O'Connell was invited to speak. O'Connell became a member of the BPU and Attwood felt his presence gave it added credibility. The Catholic Association was already under way in Ireland, and its activities provided them with an ideal role model.[14]

---

10 Hopkins, *ibid.*, p.88.
11 Kesteven, *Triumph*, p.49; *Oxford Dictionary of Biographies*, online version, p.4, accessed 20/09/19; Prime Ministers during this period were: Duke of Wellington, 1828-1830; Earl Grey 1830-34; Viscount Melbourne July 1834 – November 1834; Duke of Wellington November 1834 – December 1834; Sir Robert Peel December 1834 – April 1835.
12 Garnett, *Co-operation*, p.54.
13 Hopkins, *Birmingham*, p.150.
14 Flick, *Political Union*, p.17.

Street Commissioners

The backdrop to the building of the Town Hall in Birmingham was an Act of 1769 which formalised the creation of a body termed the Birmingham Improvement Commissioners. Sometimes known as simply the Improvement or Pavement Commissioners, they are herein referred to as Street Commissioners (the sub-committee delegated to the building of the Town Hall). This title is particularly apt considering the importance of road travel to the commercial livelihood of the town. The main group initially comprised fifty members, one of the first being Dr John Ash of the Birmingham General Hospital. Members were unpaid, unelected and largely self-selected. Their remit was broad, gradually extending to something akin to the Local Authorities of today. Widening, maintenance and latterly surfacing of streets were key factors to Birmingham's success, most notably New Street. This was extended to the provision of street names and house numbering, as well as street lighting and control of overhanging signs. Even after Birmingham became the hub of a major canal network, transport by this means was slow and roads were still important, both across and in and out of the town. An underlying priority was to ensure the efficient and effective management of central markets. Situated in the centre of the country, supplies of raw materials and communication with potential customers were crucial to their success. The clearance of obstructions and removal of refuse was also one of their functions, as was the establishment of a basic form of policing. Membership of the Committee was not popular and meetings were often adjourned due to the inadequate number of attendees.[15] This could, in part, be the cause of the slow progress with regard to arrangements for the Town Hall.

However, on completion and following the success of the Town Hall, a similar thirst for aggrandisement, beyond basic maintenance, prompted a new Market Hall and the replacement of the Grammar School. The Market Hall was designed by the Birmingham architect Charles Edge, at an astronomical cost of £67,261. The Commissioners remained in force after the Municipal Corporations Act of 1835, gradually relinquishing their role to the new corporation following the Birmingham Improvement Act of 1851.

Choice of site

A site on the corner of Waterloo Street and Bennetts Hill down to New Street and opposite the Public News Room was originally chosen. Advertisements were placed for plans, specifications and estimates. However, disagreements arose between the Committee and the vendors of the site, who wanted either to reduce the size of the plot from 2,550 sq.yds to 2,200, or to increase the

---

15 Hopkins, *Birmingham*, p.141.

purchase price from £6,700 to £7,500. The Committee objected, saying that the cost was already double that originally envisaged, but the Music Society urged them to reconsider, saying that to lose the site for the sake of £800 would be a shame when the benefits were likely to be so great. Unlike the proactive Music Society, the Street Commissioners were somewhat dilatory, and nearly a year passed before they admitted that negotiations had broken down. They then looked at a site in Ann Street (now Colmore Row) but this was far too expensive. The present site, between Paradise Street and Congreve Street, was finally agreed, at a cost of £7,000. This was not without some wheeling and dealing, as two of the Committee members had purchased plots on the site. In August 1830 two more members were added to the Committee and Samuel Galton was appointed Treasurer. Galton was a Quaker and gun-maker who had previously endowed thirty additional beds to the General Hospital.[16] Several of the short-listed entries for the competition, including Hansom's, were too large and had to be adjusted and resubmitted. This meant that he had to encroach over the footpath pavement and was unable to provide an imposing entry, with steps. He did, however, succeed in enhancing the visual impact of height by the use of a rusticated basement. His prime objective was for the concert area to be as large as possible. The nominal capacity was 3,500, but far greater if seating was removed. It was ironic that, having laid strict restrictions upon the size of the site, and after Hansom had left, the Street Commissioners gave way to the Music Society and agreed to an extension, giving extra space for a Hill's organ.[17] The Society raised funds for this, and the organ remained their property.[18]

PEOPLE

Attwood and O'Connell were contemporaries of Owen, thus Hansom was operating under their shadow. Attwood's main platform was the full force of the Birmingham Political Union, of which William Pare was a leading member. Pare was the same age as Hansom.

Thomas Attwood

Thomas Attwood was not a member of the organising Committee, but his contribution, not just in financial terms, cannot be underestimated. His original objections to political reform, especially that which permitted men to sit in Parliament 'without the qualification of property', changed along with social conditions, when he began to acknowledge the need for the middle classes and growing towns such as Birmingham and Manchester to be represented. Thus, in 1816 he published the first of seven pamphlets on

---
16 Hopkins, *ibid.*, p.141.
17 Made by William Hill, the famous organ-maker, the organ was the largest in England at the time.
18 The extension was not built by Hansom, but by Edge.

monetary reform. He argued that the lack of available money limited the purchasing power of the population, which in turn artificially restricted the level of production. This provided a platform for his argument for a cross-class alliance between employers and workers, where both stood to gain with higher profits on the one hand, and higher wages on the other. He singled out the East India Company, whose policy of restricting foreign trade he believed was adding to the growing unemployment in Birmingham. He led a delegation from the town, which gave evidence to a Select Committee, and succeeded in persuading the House of Commons to restrict the Company's monopoly.[19] This led to his theory based upon the use of paper currency which was not linked to gold, a way of increasing supply and helping to reduce unemployment. However, despite considerable local support, backed by a petition signed by some 40,000 people, he failed to win over central Government. His somewhat unconventional views on monetary reform had to be advanced independently, and it was here that he joined forces with Robert Owen. Some reports suggest that it was Hansom who brought Owen to Birmingham, though Attwood, and then Pare, also wrote to him.[20]

Disappointed with the minimal extent of change brought about by the Great Reform Bill, Attwood attempted to revive the BPU and gain support for his monetary reform.[21] Anxious not to break the law, he sought advice from O'Connell and other eminent lawyers.[22] He then attempted to emulate O'Connell's scheme of charging members a subscription of a penny a week, but the lower classes were not prepared to do this, and expected the middle-classes to finance their own cause.[23] The appointment of collectors did not solve the problem. A meeting was called at which Attwood needed to ensure a large sympathetic audience.[24] He began by giving a few words of praise for the Irish Catholics. This gave the Catholic priest Thomas McDonnell an entrée. Always a potential source of trouble, even when a supporter, McDonnell commenced with an attack on the English aristocracy.[25] O'Connell's position was more on the political front. He claimed that he would go on bended knee in support of anyone trying to prevent Conservative supremacy.[26] He held a meeting in the Town Hall and tried to persuade the audience that they should support the Whigs, stating that this would help both Ireland and England.[27] The meeting was heralded by flags and banners, and a grand procession

---

19 Hopkins, *Birmingham*, p.145.
20 Podmore, biography, p.430; Postgate, *Builders' History*, p.91; Barnsby, *Working People*, p.62.
21 Flick, *Political Union*, p.14.
22 Flick, *ibid.*, p.43.
23 Flick, *ibid.*, pp.37-38.
24 Moss, *Attwood*, p.159.
25 Moss, *ibid.*
26 Flick, *Political Union*, p.111.
27 Moss, *Attwood*, p.274.

which included an open carriage with Attwood and O'Connell hailed as honoured guests: 'the Liberators of England and Ireland'. This resulted in a petition which O'Connell presented to the House of Commons on their behalf. However the number of attendees at the meeting was far less than at previous events. It didn't have support from surrounding areas and many Birmingham employers refused permission for their workers to attend. By then the economy was improving, the need was coming to an end and the moment had passed.

William Pare
Not only was Attwood's contribution significant, but also that of William Pare, an established tobacco and cigar retailer based in New Street. The part he played tends to be understated, largely because he never sought personal notoriety, though this doesn't entirely explain it as he was a prolific writer and lectured widely across the country. Garnett, however, faithfully records his every participation, from his teenage years through to late in life.[28]

Pare was first inspired by the Newhall Meetings of 1819, and then subsequent visits to Ralahine. Reputedly wealthy, and more down-to-earth than Owen, his commercial enterprises never interrupted his political interests or his loyalty to his home town.[29] Together with two publishers, James Guest and William Hawksworth Smith, he set up the Birmingham Co-operative Society. A year later, in 1829, he became President.[30] Owenism, founded on principles which emanated from New Lanark, was, therefore, already well underway by the time Owen and Hansom arrived in Birmingham. The aims and objects of the Society were that:

> nothing shall in the way of profits and trade, or any part of the capital, shall ever be divided among the Members, a Community of property in Land and Goods is the great object.[31]

Pare also became editor of the *Birmingham Co-operative Herald,* and Secretary of the Mechanics Institute, of which Attwood was Treasurer and Spooner, his partner, was President.[32] He tried to combine Owen's vision of 'self-help with profits' and Attwood's concerns as to 'inefficient currency' with his own leaning towards the setting up of communities. A report of the proceedings of the Second Co-operative Congress 1831 states that:

---

28 See Garnett, R.G., *Co-operative Review,* 'William Pare: A non-Rochdale Pioneer', May 1964.
29 Moss, *Attwood*, p.156.
30 Garnett, 'Rochdale Pioneer', p.145.
31 Garnett, *Co-operation,* p.145.
32 Flick, *Political Union*, p.167.

the first sales of co-operative milk were at Birmingham, by an unemployed co-operator for whom members of the Birmingham Co-operative Society subscribed 6d. and purchased milk cans, yoke and pony; the Society paid him 15s. weekly, 'all out of profits, arising from the sale of Co-operative milk'.[33]

At one stage Pare suggested the possibility of a bartering arrangement between Irish farm produce and Birmingham hardware.[34] At his farewell dinner, he was acclaimed as the 'most active reformer in Birmingham after Attwood'.[35] When his political activities became an embarrassment to his new post as Registrar of Births and Marriages, he was obliged to resign. Having firstly sold £500 railway shares, Pare's family was to be one of those which subsequently relocated to Hampshire. Brought in to sort out some of its financial difficulties, he eventually became acting governor.

Rev Thomas M McDonnell

Another unsung hero of the Owen and Hansom phase in Birmingham was the incongruous intervention of Hansom's parish priest, Father Thomas McDonnell. Taking advantage of other changes in Birmingham, McDonnell set out to 'put his Birmingham congregation on the map'.[36] At first he was very popular locally and increased the size of his congregation three-fold, but he went out of favour with his Catholic authorities when he became a vociferous member of the BPU. For a time he was a Council member and spoke at many public meetings.[37] This was deemed quite inappropriate for a priest. His political platform started as a campaign against pew rents, a divisive system whereby fees had to be paid, leaving the less well off to occupy free seats, located at the back of churches where it was difficult to follow the proceedings. Furthermore, paid seats were often left empty. The contentious pew rent situation was largely with the Established Church, that is the Church of England, not in Catholic or other dissenting churches. Though not of Irish birth, the question of pew rents was particularly problematic in Ireland. Not dissimilar to that of English pew rents, where mainly absentee Irish landlords emulated English gentry, the Irish were required to contribute tithes to the government towards the funding of the Irish Anglican Church.[38]

---

33 Thompson and Williams, *Legacy,* p.160 quoting *Lancashire Cooperator,* 6 August 1831.
34 Garnett, *Co-operation,* p.114 quoting letter Pare from Dublin to managers of Birmingham Equitable Labour Exchange, 3 October 1833.
35 Garnett, *ibid.,* p.175.
36 Champ, Judith, F., 'Assimilation and Separation: the Catholic Revival in Birmingham c1640-1850' unpublished doctoral thesis, University of Birmingham, 1984, p.162 quoting 'The Case of the Rev T.M. McDonnell stated by himself in a series of letters' (1842), p.29.
37 Champ, 'Assimilation', p.172.
38 Atkins, D.H., *The Church of Ireland: Ecclesiastical Reform and Revolution, 1800-1885* (Newhaven and London, 1971).

Despite comprising seventy-five percent of the mainly peasant population, Irish Catholics were treated as a minority, and also expected to relinquish ten per cent of their agricultural produce. As Unions urged workers in England to withhold their services by going on strike, McDonnell urged Catholics in Ireland to abstain from paying rents. This was a hostile and confrontational course of action, incompatible with Owen and Attwood's calls for peace.

McDonnell was an ardent admirer of O'Connell.[39] He had already invited him to speak to his congregation in 1825, and did so again just as the political upheavals of 1832 began to escalate. McDonnell became the editor of the *Catholic Magazine*, and used it to air his views, however he was forced to resign early in 1833 after refusing to pay a debt which he had incurred for the union for an unauthorised public entry given to O'Connell.[40] McDonnell had a tendency to be surrounded by controversy. He was unashamedly outspoken in his views and overplayed his hand when, in 1839, he started to condemn the proposed new police body and watch committee, which he felt were 'imposing unconstitutional force in the town'.[41] He subsequently left Birmingham, to take up a post in the West Country.

Daniel O'Connell and Ireland

An Irish thread runs throughout, from visits by Owen and Pare to the community at Ralahine, and Owen's many speeches in the magnificent Dublin Rotunda.[42] Even Pare's later years were spent in Ireland, when he lived in Dublin between 1846 and 1865, working as the manager of an ironworks. Unrest in Ireland was as bad, if not worse than in England. Motivation behind the Ralahine community was as much a way for the owner, John Scott Vandeleur, to protect his workforce from violence as any devotion to Owenite principles.[43]

When the French Revolution broke out, O'Connell was one of the many Catholics forced to abandon his studies for the priesthood at the English College, a major seminary in Douai. He then trained as a lawyer, and entered Lincoln's Inn in 1794.[44] Like Attwood, O'Connell was at heart a reformer, seeking an Irish Parliament, though without complete separation from England. He saw Catholic emancipation as the first step towards this. It was a means of quelling any possible Irish Rebellion rather than a conscious bias towards Catholics.[45] The success of the Association was considered a threat, and closed by the Irish authorities. However, also like Owen, O'Connell kept forming new associations under different names.

---

39 Champ, 'Assimilation', p.170.
40 Moss, *Attwood,* p.245.
41 Champ, 'Assimilation', p.178.
42 Royle, *millennium,* p.52.
43 Royle, *ibid.,* p.52.
44 Woodward, E.L., *The Age of Reform* (Oxford, 1938), p.326.
45 Kestven, *Triumph*, pp.39, 40.

The majority of the Irish population joined O'Connell's Association, the first democratic mass movement in the world. Inspired by the French attitude towards *liberté* and *égalité*, the main mission of the Association was to campaign against the control the English government held over Ireland.[46] O'Connell used it when campaigning for his right to sit in Parliament. He defeated the standing member in a bye-election in County Clare, but was still not allowed to hold a seat in the House of Commons.[47] Forced to stand for re-election, which he won, he then became the first Irish Member. Having succeeded, one of his objectives was also to campaign for the building of new Catholic churches across England. In 1842 he took part in a 'Grand [fund-raising] Meeting' in Liverpool attended by five thousand people.[48] The following year he was invited by Hansom to talk in Gravesend, where he raised £100 in support of the church of St Gregory the Great which he built to serve Polish seamen.[49]

POLITICS

Thompson and Williams argue that trade unions and societies were interchangeable.[50] Indeed, to unscramble the similarities, the differences and the inter-relationship between the Equitable Labour Exchanges of the middle-class radicals and their Labour Notes, the GNCTU, and even the influence of the working-class Birmingham Political Union, would be a separate exercise in itself, and not entirely relevant to the Owen-Hansom scenario. However, they cannot be ignored as they were an integral part of the general upheaval at this time and both men were involved to some degree. The question of class was another emotive subject and had been debated at the 1833 Congress. The press was sceptical:

> Independent Co-operation cannot be successfully established in this country – even as an experiment – till the working classes obtain their political rights …. Mr Owen is benevolently disposed to do his utmost to better the condition of mankind, but he exhibits strange perversity of mind in expecting to realise his political millennium before working men are placed on an equal footing with other classes of community with regard to political rights.[51]

When Owen returned from America in June 1828, he discovered that some of his former ideas about co-operative working had been transmuted into trade unions. He was still giving lectures and trying to 'change the world' by

---

46 McDowell, R.B., 'The Protestant Nation 1775-1800' in Moody, T.W. and Martin, F.X. (eds.), *The Course of Irish History* (New York, 1967), pp.236, 245.
47 Pare described Clare as a particularly unruly area, Garnett, *Co-operation,* p.105.
48 *Freeman's Journal & Daily Commercial Advertiser,* 13 August, 1842.
49 Mansfield, F.A., *The History of Gravesend in the County of Kent* (Rochester, 1981 reprint), p.114.
50 Thompson, and Williams, *Legacy,* p.160.
51 *Poor Man's Guardian*, 14 January 1832.

means of communities, but was temporarily thrown off course by the way things had evolved in his absence. The unions were already campaigning for shorter working hours, less child labour and better conditions, generally as he had done when he was in New Lanark. It was now that he started up the Labour Exchanges, similar to those which Thomas Attwood was promoting in Birmingham. This was a scheme whereby goods could be exchanged between Co-operative Societies, and Labour Notes were given out, measured in value by the number of hours a person had worked, essentially cutting out middlemen.

Birmingham Political Union
Firstly, it is necessary to back-track a little. Attwood's main interest was monetary reform, Hansom's was fairer working and living conditions, especially for builders, and Owen was interested in shorter working hours and reducing child labour in factories. When approached initially by Attwood, and then by Pare, Owen declined to become a member as he was not directly political at that time.[52] At his speech in December 1832, Owen referred to the 'existing ignorance, poverty and degradation of a large portion of the industrious classes' and the sufferings of the people under the 'present accursed system [monetary as well as social]', thus bringing all these different strands together.[53]

A more comprehensive description of the BPU than that already given, comes from Garnett, namely a society to provide 'mutual protection against poverty' and 'independence through growth of common capital'.[54] This would be achieved by means of weekly subscriptions of 4d, trading/manufacturing operations and community settlement. Like at New Lanark, members were expected to purchase goods from their own store. The list of members given by Pare gives an informed picture of the more prominent types of trade which were being carried out in the town:

> Brass founders, jewellers, silversmiths, japanners, platers, gilt-toy makers, wire-workers, button-makers, screwdrivers, saddlers, hot-house manufacturers, rulemakers, gun-makers, engravers, wood-turners, book-binders, pocket-book makers, Britannia metal workers, shoe-makers, tailors, millers, bakers, etc.[55]

Attwood's meetings were highly organised. To gain maximum appeal, he called his meetings 'Great Meetings of all Inhabitants'.[56] A record of his speech

---
52 Podmore, *biography*, pp.429-430.
53 Mr Owen's Address, *Birmingham Journal*, 8 December 1832.
54 Garnett, *Co-operation*, p.53.
55 Letter Pare to *Weekly Free Press*, 11 August 1830.
56 Reekes, *Speeches*, p.14.

was published, with a lengthy title: 'Report of the Proceedings of the Great Meeting of the Inhabitants of the Midlands Districts held at Birmingham, 7 May 1832, convened by the Council of the Political Union for the purpose of Petitioning the House of Lords to pass the Reform Bill'. The scale and peaceful nature of the meeting was an attempt to both gain acceptability and put on pressure. The date was appropriately chosen as a Monday, for maximum attendance. Newhall Hill was transformed into an amphitheatre. It was bedecked with blue pro-Reform ribbons and BPU medals were worn by spectators.[57] The day did indeed pass off peacefully, and the fear of infiltration from people brought in to incite violence proved unfounded.[58]

Political Unions in both Bromsgrove and Worcester were particularly active. Not being able to defend himself from the inevitability of a negative outcome with the Town Hall, Hansom did, nevertheless have supporters within the ranks of the Street Commissioners. When they dismissed him, their treasurer, Samuel Tertius Galton, resigned in sympathy. It was through Galton that he acquired the job of erecting the Bromsgrove Lickey Memorial to commemorate the late Earl of Plymouth. Galton was the brother of John Howard, Deputy Lieutenant and High Sheriff of Worcester in 1834. The memorial was built of Anglesey marble, and work was superintended by Welch's younger brother, John.

Labour Notes
Owen had a very high opinion of Birmingham, saying that it was the most forward-thinking city in the country, and that 'the country owed reform to Birmingham, and its salvation from revolution'.[59] Attracted by its vibrant entrepreneurial activities and its overtly radical society, he progressed his scheme for Labour Notes, whereby notional working hours were used as a measure of trade, rather than the gold currency which Attwood decried. A form of labour notes had already been used in New Lanark, and also in Indiana. It was not a new idea. At New Lanark, rather than using coins, which were in short supply, Owen paid for work by means of 'Tickets for Wages', whereby the value of work could be used to purchase goods, in this case in his shop. This was a shrewd move, as it also provided additional income for Owen.[60] Labour Notes were trialled in America, and in Birmingham Pare actively promoted their use, having seen how successful they were at Ralahine.[61] They

---

57 Reekes, *ibid.*, p.15.
58 Flick, *Political Union,* p.79.
59 Peers, *Town Hall,* p.15 (14): Briggs, quoting p.190 from *Personal Life of George Grote* in 'Thomas Attwood and the economic background of the Birmingham Political Union', *Cambridge Historical Journal* vol.1, x, no.2 (London, 1948).
60 Donnachie, *Owen of New Lanark,* p.172.
61 Garnett, R,G., 'Robert Owen and the Community Experiments' in Pollard, Sidney and Salt, John, (eds.) *Robert Owen Prophet of the Poor* (London and Basingstoke, 1971), p.50.

were an indirect attack on capitalists, a means of circumventing the existing form of currency, hopefully making it redundant.[62] In Hopkins' opinion, their introduction may have encouraged more people to join the BPU.[63] They were issued through National Equitable Labour Exchanges. At the end of the first year the Birmingham branch claimed to have made a profit of £200.[64] However, the collapse of the short-lived GNCTU brought them to an end.[65] No further notes were issued after May 1834.[66]

Equitable Labour Exchanges

Owen had toyed with the idea of labour exchanges at New Lanark back in 1820.[67] The radical stirrings of Birmingham in 1832 led him to establish two official Exchanges, one in London and one in Birmingham, vehicles through which labour notes could be issued. Whereas Attwood hoped paper money would increase purchasing power and reduce unemployment, Owen took this a stage further and hoped that goods could now be exchanged directly, his main aim being to cut out the middleman.[68] Competition would be negated and money raised for communities, as Owen claimed that 'They (the workers) can each produce more than they have occasion for themselves, and they are each in want of each other's surplus produce' – a manifesto for a community?[69] At local level, the Exchanges were publicised by means of the *Birmingham Labour Exchange Gazette,* founded in January 1833. It attracted thousands of artisans. Valuing labour and goods proved problematic, but Owen was confident that there was a 'scientific' way of achieving this.[70] He devised a 'time standard' and published lengthy guide-lines in *The Crisis*.[71] In essence, an average ten-hour day's labour was estimated to be 6d per hour. The value of raw materials would be added to the value of hours worked, and the total divided by 6d. This would give the number of hours to be quoted on the labour note. However, from this 1d in the shilling was deducted by way of commission. Thus, the Labour Exchange was acting as an unofficial middleman, albeit taking an amount considerably less than its predecessors. Despite this, the concept was so popular that branches were inundated with goods. It was not unusual for them to have to close their doors to allow time to value the items.

---

62 Thompson and Williams, *Legacy*, p.159.
63 Hopkins, *Birmingham*, p.145.
64 Garnett, *Co-operation*, p.140.
65 Garnett, *ibid.,* p.142.
66 *The Crisis*, 31 May 1834.
67 Donnachie, *Owen of New Lanark*, p.259.
68 Barnsby, *Working People*, p.45.
69 Donnachie, *Owen of New Lanark*, p.259; Podmore, *biography*, p.405; *The Crisis* June 1832.
70 See Harrison, John, 'Robert Owen and the Communities', in 'Robert Owen, Industrialist, Reformer, Visionary 1771-1858', pp.27-32.
71 Podmore, *biography*, p.407: *The Crisis,* vol.1, pp.59, 60.

The first Labour Exchange (June 1832) was set up in Gray's Inn Road, a substantial property where Owen was living at the time.[72] After that it moved to Fitzroy Square. When the Birmingham branch was established, ten members of the committee were BPU members, but Attwood was not one of them.[73] Owen was Governor. As happened later on at Harmony Hall, financial records were less than efficient and the London branches fell into difficulties. The demise of the Birmingham Exchange was in part due to lack of support, but also closely linked to the demise of the GNCTU. All debts and the original share capital were repaid, with the remaining funds of £8.3s.1/2d. being donated to the General Hospital Fund.[74] It was the only branch to close voluntarily and the only one to have made a profit.

Grand National Consolidated Trades Union of England and Ireland
Their experiences over the Grammar School had taught Owen and Hansom that the Builders' Union would never be sufficiently powerful on its own. It needed to be part of a much larger union, made up of existing societies and covering workers of all kinds. In February 1834 the former *Journal* of the Builders' Union became *The Pioneer,* promoting the newly formed GNCTU and presenting things from a wider Owenite perspective. James Morrison, a painter from Newcastle with 'literary yearnings', moved to Birmingham and took over editorship.[75] He wrote to Owen asking him to contribute to the first edition, saying that Hansom and Welch had already agreed to do so.[76] Hansom acted briefly as deputy-editor. The GNCTU was a rather nebulous organisation, grand only in name, and something which proved not to be as all-inclusive as its title implied.[77] Much to Owen and Hansom's annoyance, the builders were not entirely supportive of the idea and Owen initially kept at a distance. However, membership rose very fast and the builders were totally overshadowed by the vast scale of the larger union. The whole make or break future of unions in general lay in balance. If the Consolidated Union was not a success, then the Builders' Union would go down with it – and the builders were already struggling. They lost the battle in Lancashire and joiners and bricklayers in Manchester started to lobby for its dissolution.

The organisation was not initiated by Owen, but by James (or John), Doherty.[78] Born in Ireland, and working as a cotton spinner at the age of ten years, Doherty migrated to Manchester in 1816. His role in the spinners'

---

72 Podmore, *biography,* p.405.
73 Hopkins, *Birmingham,* pp.145, 146.
74 Podmore, *biography,* p.420.
75 Harrison, *Owenites in Britain,* p.209.
76 Morrison to Owen, 2 September 1833, RO.O. 659.
77 Garnett, *Co-operation,* p.53.
78 See Butt, John, 'Robert Owen and Trade Unionism', in 'Robert Owen, Industrialist, Reformer, Visionary 1771-1858', pp.15-19.

strike led him to be imprisoned for two years. On his release he joined the Amalgamated Association of Operative Cotton Spinners and was duly elected leader of the Manchester Spinners Union. This led to a six-month strike, where, like at Derby, strikers were forced back to work to avoid starvation. Doherty wanted his Lancashire-based National Association for the Protection of Labour to move to London, but failed to get sufficient support. Local arguments prompted his resignation. Long working hours and the use of child labour became an increasingly big issue, not just in Lancashire, but across the whole country. These, together with protecting wages and improved working conditions, were the deciding factors upon which the GNCTU was launched.[79] The initial membership of half a million quickly rose to one million. Morrison, as editor of *The Pioneer*, dramatically claimed 'Our little snowballs have all been rolled together and formed into a mighty avalanche'.

Government saw the GNCTU as a direct attack on capitalists and they carefully monitored its activities. They made a quick move by making an example of the uprising of seven agricultural labourers in Dorset, who became known as the Tolpuddle Martyrs. The men refused to renounce membership of their local branch of the GNCTU as a condition of employment and were duly deported to Australia. This accelerated the collapse of the GNCTU, which, despite the furore it raised, only lasted five months. It became so contentious that some employers would only give work to those who signed oaths formally renouncing membership.

Neither Owen nor Hansom approved of strikes and Owen was no Trade Union organiser.[80] When discussing the Equitable Labour Exchanges and the GNCTU, Margaret Cole said that Owen 'was as bad a leader as could have been found'.[81] He hoped it would replace the capitalist society, and at first he tried to remain independent. It was at this stage that he set up his newspaper called *The Crisis,* but he got dragged into the GNCTU when he was invited to become Grand Master. However his popularity was already beginning to wane nationally and he was ostracised further from parliamentary circles following the spectacular and very public rise and fall of the GNCTU. This was, in part, due to funds having been drained in order to finance strikers in the Derby Lockout. Owen's attempt to secure a parliamentary enquiry regarding clemency for the Tolpuddle Martyrs failed, and his fleeting interest in the working classes, with whom he had had very little direct contact, came to an end.[82]

---

79 Thompson and Williams, *Legacy,* p.159.
80 Claeys, *Selected Works,* p.88.
81 Cole, Margaret, 'Owen's Mind and Methods', in Pollard, *Prophet,* p.211.
82 Thompson and Williams, *Legacy,* p.144, (92): *UCL* Brougham MSS Owen to Brougham, 24 February, 18 May, 19 July 1834; *Times* 15 August 1834; also pp.167-168.

Despite Hansom's efforts and those of Thomas Attwood, the age-old gap between employers and employees was too wide and the Union did not have the funds to support the strikes it advocated. Therefore by August it had folded, bringing down many small co-operative shops and his own newspaper, as well as the labour exchanges. Owen went on to continue his work in other ways, forming the Association of All Classes and All Nations and a whole string of others, giving regular lectures and setting up a new newspaper called *New Moral World*. This lasted from 1834, the year of Hansom's bankruptcy, through to 1845. The Association of All Classes led to the Universal Community Society of Rational Religionists. The final denouement of this episode is depicted in the next chapter, when Owen, Pare, the Religious Rationalists and many others were coerced into relocating to the remote Hampshire countryside.

17. Engraving of Birmingham from the South, drawn by W. Harvey, showing Town Hall on horizon

18. Thomas Attwood reclining on steps outside Town Hall

THE MEETING ON NEWHALL HILL, MAY 7TH, 1832.
(From *Cassell's History of England*.)

19. Newhall Hill Meeting

20. Bromsgrove Lickey Memorial

21(a). Rational Medals

21(b). National Equitable Labour Exchange Note

CHAPTER IV

NEW BEGINNINGS –

Owen's millennium

EARLY COMMUNITIES
During his final four years at New Lanark, Owen pondered on his idea of a community and devoted much time to fund-raising. While he was away in America, his ideas were tried out in England by others. The first attempt was the Co-operative and Economical Society, a group of London printers where twenty-one families lived together at Spa Fields, Clerkenwell.[1] Like Owen, it equated the value of labour with the selling of goods. However, it was not self-supportive financially by this means, in that the printers continued with their regular employment. It survived for two years, between 1821 and 1823. The second group was established at Motherwell, not far from New Lanark, but it barely began and was reconstituted at nearby Orbiston, where it survived until 1827. In both cases, the land was owned by General John Hamilton of Dalzell. His son, Archibald James, along with Abram Combe, were the instigators. Among the donors were A.J. Hamilton, who gave £5,000, and Sir Isaac Lyon Goldsmid, the owner of the Hampshire property which Owen

---

1 Royle, *millennium,* pp.28, 49.

ultimately leased.² History is monotonously repetitive, with debts mounting and in-fighting taking place. In this case, it was compounded by the death of Combe, the wealthy tanner from Edinburgh who became a trustee.³ Owen donated £10,000, but he had no direct involvement in the running of the community.

Perhaps the community which most influenced Owen was Ralahine in County Clare. This community was based on agriculture rather than the mills of New Lanark or the commercial enterprises of New Harmony. Owen believed in spade agriculture, for he disapproved of the plough, and agriculture was the intended main source of income for his community at Tytherley. Ralahine was set up by its owner, John Scott Vandeleur, a wealthy capitalist and philanthropist who was also an advocate of Owenite principles. His motivation was, however, also linked to the social conditions in Ireland and was as much a means of protecting his workforce from violence as any other. He had been inspired by the First Co-operative Congress in Salford which he attended, as had Pare, and his community flourished when first established. It comprised an estate of 618 acres and was managed by E.T. Craig from Manchester on similar lines to New Lanark. It only collapsed when Vandeleur lost all his money through gambling debts.⁴

Before Owen could progress his theories, he was up-staged by a book on communities published by Thompson in 1830.⁵ Carrying this to extremes, Owen's master 'Plan' was a millennial re-shaping of mankind, not in the religious or calendrical sense which Rapp had preached at New Harmony, but in global, far-reaching terms. It was so extensive that he even talked of flattening the world so that each community could link easily with others.⁶ His unswerving dedication to his 'truth' was consistent throughout his life. He never changed from his original ideal, as first outlined in his 1817 Report to the County of Lanark, and later presented to the Archbishop's committee and again to the Select Committee of the House of Commons on the Poor Laws.⁷ His audiences were dumbfounded by the enormity of the scale which he outlined, and overwhelmed with the minutiae of detail he had prepared, but perhaps no-one more so than Owen himself, for when the time finally came to put his theories into practice, he lost confidence and hesitated. As Garnett pointed out, he had difficulty in following through the practical

---

2 Royle, *ibid.,* p.28.
3 Cole, *Robert Owen,* p.174; Garnett, *Co-operation,* pp.67, 87.
4 Cole, *Robert Owen,* p.176.
5 Thompson, William, *Practical Directions for the Speedy and Economical Establishment of Communities, on the Principles of Mutual Co-operation, United Possessions and Equality of Exertions and of the means of Enjoyments.*
6 Morton, *Life and Ideas* (London, 1962), pp.120-121.
7 Royle, *millennium,* p.26.

implications of his policies.⁸ It was George Alexander Fleming and James Rigby, two of his most ardent supporters, who finally induced him to proceed. Rigby was a former delegate from the Birmingham Builders' Union.⁹ The Salford Congress was unanimous that 'it was desirable that a Community, on the principle of Mutual Co-operation, United Possessions, and Equality of Exertions and of the Means of Enjoyment', should be established as quickly as possible. However, subscriptions and membership were falling off, as without any sign of an actual community being formed, enthusiasm was waning. At first reluctant to embark on the implementation of his 'Plan', Owen finally agreed. Having invested and lost his substantial personal capital in America, lack of funding, another constant theme, plagued the scheme. The first priority was, of course, to find a suitable site, but this was only part of a bigger picture. There were negative forces going on behind the scenes, which had led firstly to Pare being pushed out of his position of Registrar in Birmingham, and then a major uproar which followed them down to Hampshire.

Nevertheless, in the wake of the huge and lasting impact which Hansom had upon the Builders' Guild and the Trade Union movement, combined with the benefit of Birmingham's central location, Owen continued to campaign in the city after Hansom had left. In 1838 the Manchester Congress transferred its Headquarters to Birmingham and in 1839 a Socialist Congress was held there, lasting for sixteen days.¹⁰ Owen had wanted it to be held in the Town Hall, but his reputation was tarnished by his views on religion, and the High Bailiff refused permission. An alternative venue had to be found. It was during this Congress that the socially propagandist Association of All Classes of All Nations and the community-minded National Community Friendly Society joined forces. They combined to form the Universal Community Society for Rational Religionists. It was also during this Congress that a report was given of sites considered suitable for the establishment of a community.¹¹ Trips were taken to East Anglia, mainly in the Downham Market area, but none of them were satisfactory. They did make an offer for one of the properties, but the vendor changed his mind.¹² As will be seen, the site they eventually chose was also unsuitable. Nevertheless, a decision was made to purchase Queen Wood Farm, at a remote location on the outskirts of East Tytherley in Hampshire, some twelve miles from Salisbury. The Rational Religionists gave sufficient financial support for the project to proceed. On one occasion

---

8 Garnett, *Co-operation*, p.14.
9 Rigby was a former delegate from the Birmingham Builders' Union; Duncan, Floyd, *The Utopian Prince, Robert Owen and the Search for Millennium*, (revised edition, 2004), p.2.
10 Barnsby, *Working People*, p.64.
11 Royle, *millennium*, p.95; Podmore, *biography*, pp.579-580.
12 Booth, *Socialism*, pp.206-207.

they sent a donation of £80 together with a variety of practical gifts, such as mathematical instruments, rat traps, and a patent cork screw![13]

The early days of the community were not easy, for the Religious Rationalists came under threat and there were attempts to close Tytherley. Hampshire was told to rid itself of its 'hideous [Socialist] pollution'.[14] Henry Philpotts, the Bishop of Exeter, claimed that the Society was illegal on the grounds that it had branches.[15] The clergy (McDonnell now having left Birmingham), magistrates and traders of Birmingham presented a petition to the House of Lords. It did not succeed in closing Tytherley, but it was the main reason Pare had to resign as Registrar. He was accused of using civic rooms to promote his private affairs, something he strongly disputed. John Finch, who was by then governor of Tytherley, attempted to organise counter-petitions. He tried to prove that he was a sober, God-fearing man with a poor family. Perhaps at Tytherley he became poor, but in Liverpool, Booth had described him as 'a merchant of some wealth'.[16] Furthermore, he pointed out that he had regularly lectured on teetotalism, set up a Sunday School and formed a Benefit Society. 'Is it to be supposed' he argued, 'that a man of my character would encourage any system with the remotest tendency to unchastity, immodesty or the invasion of the rights or property of others?'[17] For their part, the Religionists declared that they had registered chapels of Dissent and were, therefore permitted to collect money.

Prior to this, Finch, the nail manufacturer from Dudley turned foundry-master in Liverpool, had authored a work entitled 'The Millennium, the wisdom of Jesus and the foolery of Sectarianism'.[18] He held strong views. He had been very critical of Ralahine, stating that a typical cabin had 'no bed, no furniture, scarcely any utensil save a cast iron pot, [in] which the potatoes are boiled for the family dinner, and in which afterwards the surplus and refuse are served up to the grunters'.[19] At one stage he set up a rival society to Owen, the First Liverpool Co-operative Society, which applauded Owen's work, but at the same time denied any direct association.[20] Pare saw things at Ralahine very differently, when he wrote to the Birmingham Equitable Exchange saying: 'Our excellent friend Vandeleur, of the County of Clare, who crossed the Channel with me, is turning his attention to the establishment of a tannery for us, in his peaceful, happy and harmonious community of producers'.[21]

---

13 Barnsby, *Working People,* p.64.
14 McCabe, *Robert Owen,* p.106.
15 Barnsby, *Robert Owen and the First Socialists in the Black Country,* p.20.
16 Booth, *Socialism,* p.205.
17 Barnsby, *ibid.,* p.20.
18 Booth, *Socialism,* p.205.
19 Garnett, *Co-operation,* p.109 (41) quoting *Liverpool Mercury,* 17 March 1838.
20 Garnett, *ibid.,* p.54.
21 Letter, Co-operative College, 3 October 1833.

FROM QUEEN WOOD FARM TO HARMONY HALL

Queen Wood Farm was owned by Isaac Lyon Goldsmid, a former joint treasurer of Owen's short-lived British and Foreign Philanthropic Society.[22] It was Goldsmid's daughter, who had a special interest in Owen's educational ideas, who informed Owen that Queen Wood Farm might be available. The farm comprised 300 acres of arable land, to which adjoining acreage was added to bring it up to Owen's minimum size of 500.[23] On inspection, the farm was deemed to have been poorly managed, and much of the land was chalky, with chalk pits to both the north and south. There was also a considerable amount of flint, which Holyoake said made it 'more suited to gunsmiths'.[24] The intended farm manager, Heaton Aldam, farmer and head gardener at Whalley Hall in Derbyshire, inspected it and commented thus:

> Liable to drought. Great dependence on the weather. Too far distant from the chief Branches. Not suited to Manufactures. No Streams, or Coal. Not suited to *Spade cultivation:* wants more Capital than labour. Not sufficiently *central* in England. Will not grow white clover. The Land unnclosed [sic] and bleak.[25]

Despite dire warnings from his Trustees and his solicitor, and not wishing to lose the support of the members of the Universal Community Society, the arrangement went ahead. The deciding factor may have been that it was a leased arrangement which did not require instant capital. The cost for this was £750, the rent £350 *per annum* and the proposed number of residents 700.[26] Even though agreement had been given at Congress, Finch, who was both the first and last governor of Tytherley, stated his concerns, saying *'The [intended] estate must be in the manufacturing districts ... there the number of our best friends are to be found, capital will flow ... and we shall be able to obtain materials and dispose of our production to the greatest advantage'*.[27] This did not over-rule the decision and it went ahead regardless. Aldam was such an enthusiastic convert to Owen's principles that he was prepared to give up his prosperous position to take over this dubious prospect.

The venture was underpinned by Owen's Report and married to his experiences in America, but despite all his proselytising, his vision for Tytherley was totally nebulous. It was as if the man who had once said 'Let the business be at once set about in good earnest and the obstacles which

---

22 Royle, *millennium,* p.28.
23 Royle, *ibid.,* p.75.
24 Holyoake, *Visit,* p.7.
25 Royle, *millennium,* p.78 (67) letter Aldam to Central Board, 8 June 1839.
26 Booth, *Socialism,* p.207, *NMW* vol.vi, p.681; vol.vii. p.1219.
27 Royle, *millennium,* p.78.

now seem formidable will speedily disappear' didn't have the courage of his convictions.[28] What was the experiment trying to achieve? Was it really a 'half-way house' or 'training-place ... which for the moment should combine old ways with new' as Booth suggests?[29] Or was it simply a 'precursor', such as Hansom's precursor issue of *The Builder?* At first, Owen stood back. He had assumed that money would be forthcoming, but declined requests for him to become governor when money failed to materialise, though he did acquiesce to offering advice and recommendations.[30] Added to that, the skills of potential members were inadequate for the work which was needed, as most of them were accustomed to living in the industrial north. The community kept changing in shape and form as it struggled to survive. Harrison described it as 'a home for social misfits, or the unemployed, or people simply wanting to escape from the world', apart from reformers, of course.[31] At this stage, Owen's idea of a community could be compared to an architect, who attempted to construct a building with no foundations and no working drawings. As for a budget, this was virtually non-existent. At the 1837 Congress Owen gave a long address entitled *'Mr Owen's New Designs for Community Buildings to Accommodate All Ranks and Classes'*, stating that a sum of £60,000 was needed, to be raised through a joint stock company, and then let out on lease. An attempt was made to raise a start-up fund of £25,000, but less than ten per cent was achieved and they continued to spend what they did not have, based on the firm assumption that there *would* be a surplus to sell in the future.[32]

A rather haphazard list of gifts printed in the *New Moral World* symbolised the contributions people made:

> one new alva merino mattress with white water flock bolsters; one dozen and a half of knives and forks, with carvers; 26 quires of writing paper, one dozen and a half dessert knives and forks, two dozen lead pencils, two squares of india rubber, two sticks of indian ink, one vol. Dr Lardner's *Steam Engine,* one vol. Newton on *Vegetable Regimen,* two towels and shaving tackle; one pair of large end-irons for fireplace, one fire range, and a sieve.[33]

Whilst the philosophy behind the project was very much in line with Owen's lifelong beliefs, the buildings and environment, also inspired by Owen and

---

28 Report to New Lanark.
29 Booth, *Socialism,* p.209.
30 Cole, *New Lanark,* pp.216, 217.
31 Harrison, *Robert Owen, Reformer, Visionary,* p.30.
32 Cole, *New Lanark,* p.219.
33 Cole, *Life, Robert Owen,* p.217 n.1, *NMW,* 21 December 1839.

encouraged by his wealthy Vice-President, William Galpin, were almost the complete opposite. Margaret Cole suggests that members of Harmony Hall were not properly selected, a repeat of the same scenario in the early days of New Harmony.

FROM HARMONY HALL TO QUEENWOOD COLLEGE

Tytherley was subject to many changes. Despite having taken over stock and equipment of £1,700, Queen Wood Farm was not viable in its present form. Advertisements were placed in the *New Moral World* for both gifts and men with appropriate skills, not only for the farm, but also to build accommodation for a cottage community.[34] This would comprise a row of cottages capable of accommodating 500 people.[35] Members were selected by the Central Board, with preference being given to those who could pay £50 into the community fund.[36] Initially forty-two adults were chosen, but some left and numbers reduced to twelve adults and seven children.[37] At this stage living costs were considered to be 6s.1d per week. Most worked on gardening, farming or building, but small enterprises such as watch-making – anything where expensive equipment was not required. Women performed domestic service by rotation, so all had an equal share of labour and were placed in the same position. A wing was added to the old farm house, a very large room downstairs for dining, meetings and balls, with a sleeping area above. Finch aimed for 'a higher standard of living than that enjoyed in the outside world' and 'spared nothing in the attempt'.[38] Herein he sewed the seeds for the luxury of Owen's future Harmony Hall. Finch was an optimist, but by the end of the first winter there were still only thirty-seven adults and eight children living there, none of whom were satisfied with the living accommodation.[39] Meetings were held regularly to discuss ownership of land and equality of remuneration.[40] As the *Working Bee* tried to explain, paradise would not be instant and it would be necessary to 'put up with many inconveniences and privations at first'.[41]

Finch was particularly unpopular because of his strict teetotal regulations, though he did permit the drinking of cider made from apples in their orchard.[42] He set rigid rules, not conducive to a 'happy community', and, suffering from a temporary illness, he resigned in 1840. Charles Frederick Green, also a lessee and one of the group which had been looking at potential

---

34 Royle, *millennium*, p.84.
35 Booth, *Socialism*, p.208.
36 *NMW*, vol.vi, p.831.
37 Sixth Congress, *NMW*, vol.ix, p.315.
38 Podmore, *biography*, p.533; Royle, *millennium*, p.84.
39 Royle, *ibid.*, p.84.
40 Harrison, *Visionary*, pp.30-31.
41 *Working Bee*, 14 December 1839; *NMW*, 19 October, 1839.
42 Booth, *Socialism*, p.209; Royle, *millennium*, p.85.

sites, then took over briefly, only to be replaced by the more amenable James Rigby. When numbers were reduced further, with only thirteen adults, six children and one servant recorded in the 1841 census, there was a deficit of £533. Owen was, meanwhile, still trying to source more funding, mainly through his London-based Home Colonisation Society, which generated several large sums.[43] When the situation began to improve, Owen was again invited to become governor. This time he accepted and lived there for three years during which time he was given more-or-less unlimited powers, though it was implicit that he should not 'incur any debts unless there were at hand the means to discharge them'.[44] His level of spending was based on promises which were never fulfilled. When he resigned, or was pushed, at the end of this period, he agreed that he was liable for debts until they were discharged.

Many well-intentioned and hard-working people devoted both time and money to Tytherley, and many, like Pare, uprooted their families to serve the cause. Even the land was improving, but it was Owen's own unfettered, and slightly self-defeating, ambition to have 'nothing but the best', which determined the fate of his life-time's dream. When the farms started to make good progress, a reasonable decision was made to replace the temporary accommodation with more substantial structures. Knowing where Hansom's sympathies lay with regard to working conditions of builders, he was an obvious choice as architect for the project – buildings for residents and a school 'on the most magnificent scale'.[45] Thus began the commencement of his millennium, celebrated with the letters CM carved over the door, which Owen hoped would be 14 May 1842, the date of his 71st birthday.[46] Hansom was never part of the original plan, but with the reputation he had earned with the Town Hall in Birmingham, and then the albeit aborted Guildhall, it was natural that Owen would turn to him as the designer of his palatial pile. Regrettably there are no extant records of any instructions given by Owen, but these may well have been subject to one-to-one discussion on site. On 26 February the *NMW* reported that Owen and Hansom arrived to discuss the heating and ventilation system. Apparently these never worked properly, but it could well be that money ran out and they were outstanding features which Hansom didn't have the opportunity to complete. His Clerk of Works, if there was one, is not known.

The central building was designed using an H-plan to maximise light. It was made of red brick with a blue slate roof in the style of an elaborate Elizabethan manor house, with ornamental façade and lavish fittings throughout. An illustration of the plan is compared with that which Hansom was to use later

---

43 Booth, *Socialism*, p.210; Cole, *Robert Owen*, p.217.
44 Podmore, *biography*, p.545.
45 Podmore, ibid., p.542; Cole, *Robert Owen, New Lanark*, p.216.
46 Evinson, *Hansom*, p.131.

on for his design of the Training College for Catholic Schoolmistresses in Liverpool. The twin towers were to allow for separate entrances for single men and women to access their dormitories on the top floor.[47] The building was initially, and ironically, called 'Economy' (like Rapp's new community in Pennsylvania), but this was changed to 'Harmony' and then 'Harmony Hall'. Every facet of the three-storeyed building, even down to use of hand-made nails, was of the highest quality, and included gimmicks such as a conveyor system for dishes between kitchen and dining room, another engineering feat for Hansom. It could provide sixteen dinners at a time, and was intended to surpass most top London hotels. Even the kitchen had ornamental columns. The dining room and adjacent ballroom were sited in a semi-basement to allow more public rooms on the ground floor, the building being on a slope. They were decorated with richly finished ceilings and wainscoted with mahogany.[48] Also in the basement were capaciously arched [wine] cellars. Money seemed to be no object. The single most used descriptive adjective is 'extravagant'. This could only have been due to the later intervention of Owen and some of his wealthy supporters, for initially the building was scheduled to cost £1,500 and intended to be in true socialist/Owenite style.

Hansom is recorded as having said: '... the unity and co-operation which have existed among the workmen have contributed much to the present very advanced state of the works and will tend to greatly lessen the cost of construction'. Hansom was not one to overcharge or take advantage of his clients, and he would have appreciated the realities of the situation. His statement differs markedly from a letter published by an unknown visitor in the *Morning Chronicle,* which said 'I have heard that several of their carpenters, bricklayers, and such-like, are but indifferent workmen when put to a job'.[49] The only explanation can be that the reports were written at different stages of the work. It is indeed hoped that Hansom was paid in full for his time there, for this project was shortly to become another disaster for his philanthropist colleague, with money owing in all directions.

A similar mismatch of records is connected with Aldam, the expert farm manager who enthusiastically accepted the challenge of working on poor soil. Firstly there were complaints that [members of] the community do not cultivate the land ... and are not fitted for rough out-door work; secondly there was discontent between the resident communitarians and local outdoor labour which was brought in to assist, and thirdly between Aldam and both groups of men. Nevertheless, soil fertility was greatly enhanced by such means as manure and bone-meal, crops improved and the number of stock was increased. The working situation remained one which Aldam was unable

---

47 Royle, *millennium*, p.186.
48 Podmore, *biography*, p.543.
49 Booth, *Socialist,* p.211, n.†.

to resolve. He resigned, stating that 'it was absurd to place a man at the head of any department, if he was not allowed to manage', but the *New Moral World* preferred to claim that he had been dismissed.[50]

Landscaping was as elaborate as the house itself, with £700-£800 spent on roads, to better any built by the Romans, and promenades to allow for 2,000 visitors, even though barely 200 had visited at the time. On the assumption that more land would increase revenue, the insurge of capital was used to purchase three nearby farms, bringing the total acreage to over a thousand. As far as is known, Hansom's only recorded involvement was with the main building complex, though he may well have had some input into the layout of the grounds due to his association with Loudon in Birmingham. The yew trees at Queen Wood were so spectacular that they are frequently referenced. Loudon describes them in some detail in his book on the trees and shrubs of Britain. Known as the 'Yew Tree Walk', they were unusual in that branches met across a wide avenue so that they resembled a tunnel, or, as Podmore put it, the aisle of a cathedral.[51] Hansom's work at Tytherley seems to have come to an end in 1842, but parts were still incomplete, unfurnished and in need of more money. He may have tired of the project, been unpaid, or simply moved on. He had plenty of work elsewhere, with major projects in hand: a new convent at Princethorpe to be built in Warwickshire, and the extension of a Catholic school at Spinkhill in Derbyshire. Harmony Hall had the potential to be one of his greatest works. It was hardly a Strawberry Hill or Fontwell Abbey, where money was plentiful, but, had it survived, it would have gone down in history as a veritable Victorian folly – certainly not a parallelogram.

Briefly described as an 'Epicurean Stye', the luxurious, utopian mansion of Robert Owen, the reformer who supported the poor and wanted to change the world by achieving equality, started to show a sad state of degradation when work previously carried out by his smartly-dressed kitchen staff was taken over by the wives of the governors.[52] On his visit to Harmony Hall in 1844, George Holyoake described it as 'a stately structure ... more like Drayton Manor, the residence of Robert Peel, than the home of pioneers' – far removed from social equality. Was the reference to Drayton Manor coincidental? The original Drayton Manor was the home of Robert Peel senior, farmer and textile manufacturer from Lancashire. It was demolished and in the process of being rebuilt by his son, the future Prime Minister. The replacement Manor was designed by Sir Robert Smirke, architect of Covent Garden and one of the three original Crown, or Attached Architects. Both Owen and Hansom would have been well aware of it, in fact Hansom may have visited, as he did

---

50 Garnett, *Co-operation*, p.181; NMW, 27 May 1843.
51 Podmore, *biography*, p.531.
52 Podmore, *ibid.*, p.535.

Hatfield House on behalf of Mr Weld at Lulworth Castle.[53] As to the building work, Holyoake described the finish as having been executed with 'the most scrupulous care and thoroughness', with materials throughout being of the very best quality. His overall impression, however, was that rather than 'colonisation', it was more like 'squanderisation'. His understanding of the original remit was that it was to be one of utility, convenience and economy – a normal school, not even a community.

The story of George Rapp and his 'Harmonie' explains much about the way Owen tried to mould Harmony Hall, it explains the grapes in the garden (about which Holyoake was so disparaging), his views on marriage, the way the community was divided into departments, at the same time enforcing Owen's personal concept of millenniumism. However, he was overwhelmed by the enormity of his own ideas. His enthusiasm was pushed to extremes, so much so that during the 1842 Congress he was described by his fellows as a 'tyrant who would receive no counsel and suffer no opposition'.[54] Towards the end of his time as Governor, maybe due to an awareness of the growing financial pressures, some of his comments became inflammatory and he set his own truth above the so-called insanity of disbelievers. It was not helpful to his cause when he claimed that the 'world was a great lunatic asylum' and that 'Members of Parliament are more irrational than many of the inmates of the Middlesex County Lunatic Asylum'.[55] He was forced to give up the editorship of his newspaper when it became unacceptably overloaded with his personal views, and therefore unsaleable. A phenomena such as this was not unique to Owen, for the third editor of *The Builder* was ousted for exactly the same reason.

When the full reality of the debts he had incurred at Harmony Hall came to light, Owen had no alternative but to resign as Governor and once again Finch took over. With Owen's background, the lack of financial nouse he displayed was astonishing. In some ways, he cannot be blamed. He did, after all, hesitate to establish the community in the first instance, and it was not helped by his not having taken charge at the beginning. However, once he took over in any meaningful way, then he alone must be held responsible for the outcome. Even the local squire thought expenditure augmented by the elaborate design was unnecessary and was not surprised when it failed within five years of opening. In answer to growing complaints, Owen justified his spending by saying that he needed a property which was suitable for high-profile people from whom he hoped to receive donations. He insisted that he was setting a standard for a 'superior socialist future' and that the main building ought to be 'superior to any palace'. He may also have tried to use Hansom's reputation as 'the

---
53 *Dorset Record Office*, D/WLC/E 39/4, f.40.
54 Booth, *Socialism*, p.211.
55 *NMW*, vol.22, p.26.

architect of Birmingham Town Hall' to attract people. Owen was, of course, accustomed to a high standard of living, as he routinely accepted hospitality from many eminent personages across Great Britain and Europe. In 1840 he said that food would be 'of the very best of its kind'. It may have been once, but it deteriorated.[56] Firstly meat was no longer on offer, and towards the end some meals were reduced to bread and water. The best produce was always despatched to London for sale, with residents only given what was left over.

Schools
At the time of Holyoake's visit, there was no principal of the school in post, though the children appeared 'rubicund and happy'.[57] However, he commented that, despite being highly commendable in principle, the first priority should have been the farmsteads rather than the schools. The schools, which were intended to be an important source of revenue, progressed slowly, and the situation as he found it was not a true reflection of what had gone on before, which was mainly for adults and started in the old farm house. Tuition was quite arduous, bearing in mind that it had to fit round long working hours. On Finch's watch in 1840 maths lessons were given before work, between five until half past six. After work evening classes were offered, with dancing classes on Mondays, drawing classes followed by more dancing on Tuesdays, agriculture and botany on Wednesdays, instrumental music on Thursdays and geography and elocution on Fridays.[58] In addition to this, there was vocal music on Saturday evenings. The regimen was augmented the following year to include French, writing and arithmetic. The long-suffering workers, who were reminded of the need to be punctual for classes, were then subjected to Saturday-evening lectures on 'the principles and objects of the Rational System of Society'.[59] Music, singing and dancing were the most popular classes, especially when Albert Oestreicher took over as principal.[60] This aspect was, of course, one of the main causes of disagreement between Owen and Allen at New Lanark, yet Oestreicher considered them to be a 'powerful means towards forming the character of young people'.[61]

When Rigby was in charge, his plan for the children was initially more in the form of nursery care, with mothers taking turns to look after them, until a Nursing woman was appointed. At this stage there were only six children aged five years or under, and they were looked after in the former dining room until building work was complete. In order to develop this arrangement,

---
56 Cole, *New Lanark*, p.220.
57 Holyoake, *Visit*, p.16.
58 Royle, *millennium*, p.167.
59 *NMW*, 1 September 1842; 1 October 1842; 15 October 1842.
60 Royle, *millennium*, p.169.
61 *NMW*, 21 September 1844.

Owen then appointed a more experienced woman known to him. The system worked well, as mothers praised her for keeping the children happy – they had apparently cried a lot before her arrival. However, the arrangement didn't last long because, much to Owen's annoyance, Finch replaced her with someone of his choice. The replacement, Hanna Boyd, was paid £50 *per annum* plus board and lodging. In anticipation of the completion of building work in the main Hall, advertisements were placed in the *New Moral World* in 1842, referring to a Boarding House and Educational Establishment.[62] Fees were to be £25 *per annum*, including clothing, less any work carried out. Owen had already resigned in 1842 both as governor of the School and editor of *New Model World,* at which time no recriminations were voiced, and optimism still reigned; it was hoped that 'difficulties would be soon removed by united and energetic effort'.[63] The school started formally in 1843, at which time there were ninety-four children, thirty of whom (being children of members), paid nothing. The cost of £25 should be compared with the estimated living cost of adult residents at £37.10s.[64] Three levels of tuition were planned: an infant school for children between three and seven years, an elementary school for those between seven and fourteen, and a polytechnic, which was vocational in its approach, with emphasis on agriculture. The polytechnic never came into being. Oestreicher, who was subsequently put in overall charge of all the schools, was paid £100 *per annum*.[65] Teaching methods reflected both those in New Lanark and in the Pestalozzi schools, with a certain amount of freedom, no corporal punishment, and strong input from the pupils.

A revised prospectus was issued, but few children stayed for more than twelve months.[66] The curriculum was wide and ambitious, comprising: geography, astronomy, ancient and modern history, chemistry, anatomy and physiology, drawing, painting, vocal and instrumental music, geometry, land surveying, French and German.[67] Their day started at 5.30 am. Classes were interspersed with brief spells for boys in the workshops, farm or gardens, and the girls carrying out household duties. Some physical recreation was included. However, during 1844, when Owen was once again Governor, it became necessary to replace paid teachers, including Oestreicher, with members of the community. Even so, the schools were still running at a loss, with the cost of a boarding pupil estimated at £21.10s.3d. as against an income of £20.0s.0d.

When the disastrous financial situation could no longer be denied, attempts were made to live solely off food produced on the estate, and the missionary

---

62 *NMW,* vol.xi, 1842, p.53; Podmore, *biography,* p.546.
63 Podmore, *ibid.,* p.545.
64 Cole, *New Lanark.*
65 Royle, *millennium,* p.173.
66 Royle, *ibid.,* p.175.
67 *NMW,* 1 June 1844.

fund-raisers, who were often able men and included Green and several women, were dismissed.[68] The whole country had previously been divided into fourteen missionary districts and the missionaries often addressed large audiences in the open air. Three hundred and fifty towns were being visited regularly.[69] Their dismissal hastened the downfall of Tytherley, brought down the Rational Religionist Society and saw the end of the schools which had been planned. Right to the bitter end money was being spent on Social Halls (Halls of Science), which had to cease. Some were sold and others left incomplete.[70]

As Queenwood fell apart, Richard James Reid, one of the teachers and an outspoken critic who had by then left, delivered a report at the London Mechanic Institute. Whether true or an exaggeration, it was damning.[71] Owen's influence may have been dropping off, but he was still very well known and news of his activities spread fast. Reid said that:

> a system of vice was practised perfectly dreadful to contemplate ... vicious and indiscriminate intercourse was encouraged among the youngest members ... thieving prevailed to a frightful extent as no punishment was known for it.

He then added:

> the whole society was thoroughly corrupt and wretched, as having lost every principle of happiness and virtue, [it was] abandoned to vice, poverty, indolence and wretchedness.

More than £40,000 had been spent and the Rational Society, the umbrella organisation of the project, was bankrupted. A committee took over but couldn't cope with the seemingly insoluble difficulties. Owen's 'dream' was eventually sold to the Quaker educationalist, George Edmondson. He remained there until his sudden death in 1863. Though Hansom's building work was complete as far as was practicable, he did have a vicarious connection with the community's future, or perhaps it was more than that, perhaps he actually offered Owen a life-line. Edmondson had employed Hansom to re-order Tulketh Hall, his Lancashire property, between 1841 and 1842. The property was originally built as a Cistercian monastery, dating back to 1188, and latterly owned by the Hesketh family, Peter Hesketh being Member of Parliament for Preston at that time. At one stage Hansom confessed that he was ashamed of his work there, describing it as 'the worst he had ever done' and

---
68 Podmore, *biography,* p.544; Cole, *New Lanark,* p.218.
69 Booth, *Socialism,* p.206 quoting *NMW,* vol.vii, p.1312.
70 Booth, *Socialism,* p.212.
71 *Derby Mercury,* 23 August 1843.

saying that he had 'defaced its ancient characteristics'.[72] No clear explanation has ever been found for this comment, except inasmuch as a large number of trees was felled and put up for sale. His task was to transform the property into a school. However, Edmondson already had a proven track record and was an ideal person to take over Queenwood. He had aspired to be a teacher from the age of fourteen. He spent seven years in Russia assisting with educational and agricultural projects for the Tsar, before returning to England where he opened a school at Blackburn in Lancashire. Like Owen at New Lanark, and indeed at Harmony Hall, Edmondson encouraged a practical approach, with work shops for blacksmiths and carpenters. Further, both he and his assistant, James Simpson, followed Owen-type principles. A transcript of a lecture given by Simpson, was published in the *Preston Guardian* on 23 March 1843. It was entitled 'On the means of improving the character and condition of the working classes'. Simpson also spoke at the Liverpool Mechanics Institute, where he referred to the 'great moral movement amongst the working classes in Edinburgh, and other parts of Scotland' and said that 'to sound education alone must we look for the improvement of men's nature'.

Edmondson's Lancashire school, which he called Tulketh Hall Academy, was opened in July 1841.[73] He placed advertisements in order to recruit students:

> **GEO. EDMONDSON** Respectfully informs his Friends that his SCHOOL will OPEN on the 27 inst. – The necessary alterations and arrangements for his Pupils are now so nearly completed, that G. E. will be glad, during the remainder of the vacation, to receive the visits of any one wishing to obtain further information respecting his Establishment, than it is possible within the limits of an advertisement to convey.
>
> TERMS:- For Board, Washing, Instruction in the English, Latin, Greek, and French Languages, and Mechanical Architectural and Landscape Drawing, including Books and all other Stationery, and the use of Philosophical and Arithmetical Apparatus, £40 per Annum; Weekly Boarders £32 per Annum
>
> Under Ten Years of Age:- Yearly Boarders £35 per Annum, Weekly Boarders £27 per Annum
> PAYMENT QUARTERLY
> One vacation of six weeks at Midsummer
> (*Preston Chronicle,* 17 July 1841)

---

72 Hewitson, Anthony, *History of Preston* (Preston 1883), p.449.
73 *Manchester Times and Gazette,* 17 July 1841; *Preston Guardian,* 17 July 1841.

Similar advertisements, to reach a wider audience, were placed in *The Lancaster Gazette and General Advertiser, for Lancashire, Westmorland, &c.* The *Manchester Times* also stated that each pupil was to bring 'Four Towels'.

When Edmondson was preparing to relocate to Queenwood, Owen's former community, like New Harmony, changed direction and became more of a dedicated educational establishment. He announced his move thus:

> **QUEENWOOD COLLEGE** – HAVING VERY GENERALLY ANNOUNCED HIS INTENTION OF CHANGING HIS PRESENT RESIDENCE FOR A MORE EXTENSIVE ONE, AT THE CLOSE OF THE CURRENT HALF YEAR, GEORGE EDMONDSON wishes to lay before his Friends, and all who are interested in the subject of Education, the capabilities of his new Establishment, QUEENWOOD College, near Stockbridge, Hants, and the plans and objects which he purposes to pursue there.
>
> The possession of a Farm of upwards of eight hundred acres, the assistance of an experienced and competent Farm Superintendent, and of a talented resident Chemist, with a well-appointed Laboratory, enable him to offer many advantages to those willing to study the science and practice of Agriculture.
>
> In Civil Engineering, he will be able to give a complete course, both of office and field work, comprehending railway surveying and levelling, setting out railway curves and laying down gradients, land and estate surveying, making out plans, sections, specifications, estimates, &c., the construction of roads, canals, bridges, &c.
>
> Natural and Experimental Philosophy will hold a prominent place in the plan of instruction, a valuable collection of electrical, pneumatic galvanic, magnetic, and mechanical apparatus being provided for the use of the lecturers and their pupils.
>
> At the same time it is not G.E.'s intention to confine himself to these branches of instruction, but to furnish a good classical, mathematical, and commercial Education; and, in addition, to provide competent professors of Painting and the modern Languages.
>
> G.E.'s terms are Fifty Guineas per annum, payable half-year, in advance, for every advantage of the College, including stationery.
>
> Especially attention will be paid to Religious Instruction and the study of the Holy Scriptures.
>
> Till the 20th of 6th mo., application for the admission of Pupils, or for further information, may be made to G.E., Tulketh Hall, near Preston, Lancashire.
>
> (*Preston Guardian,* 10 July 1847)

Pupils were given access to copies of Bradshaw's Railway Time Tables and required to check routes. This slightly incongruous reference is due to the fact that Edmondson's brother Thomas was the person who devised the railway ticket system. The civil engineering section of the course was an innovative move, bearing in mind the current 'railway mania' and huge growth in the country's transport infrastructure. Before Edmondson acquired Queenwood, it was firstly put up for auction. The glowing description in the *Morning Chronicle* described it as in a high state of cultivation and richly ornamented, with the suggestion that it was suitable as an agricultural college or other public institution. It used Hansom as a selling point, saying that it was built 'in a most substantial manner' and designed by 'Mr Joseph Hansom, the architect of the Birmingham Town-Hall'. Further:

> It contained in its various departments accommodation for upwards of 150 persons, with capital dining rooms, bath rooms, library, music room and every possible convenience that can be mentioned. It was partly extra-parochial, and the poor rates on the remainder are very moderate. The Lawn is tastefully laid out, and the approaches to the Hall are planted with many hundred young trees. The Garden, which contains upwards of twelve acres, has been designed to suit the purposes of a large establishment, and is well stocked with fruit trees of all descriptions, together with a noble brick wall 500 feet in length … The roads are good, and the neighbourhood select, being in the vicinity of many gentlemen's seats. The whole property will shortly be within three miles of railway communication to all parts of the kingdom.[74]

It also stated that many thousands of pounds had been spent on the farms. Considering what a difference had been made compared with when it was first established, it is disappointing that there was not a more favourable long-term outcome from Owen's point of view. Under its new name of Queenwood College, it became both an academic and a practical establishment, with a bias towards agriculture. Whilst he was there, Edmondson made use of Owen's printing licence to establish a printing press, which produced a monthly periodical set up by the boys. This was similar to *The Tulketh Hall Mercury* which his pupils had printed at his previous school.[75] Teachers of renown under Edmondson's leadership were Dr Heinrich Debus, a German chemist; Edward Frankland, science master and chemist who was later knighted; Archer Hirst, a mathematician specialising in geometry, who went to the same school as John Tyndall, mathematics teacher and expert in land surveying

---

74 *Morning Chronicle,* 24 November 1845.
75 For first edition, see Harris Public Library.

for railways.[76] When recollecting his life in the 1840s, Tyndall alluded to the need for teachers to be able to stimulate students as well as having expert knowledge of their subject. He refers to Edmondson as a 'worthy Principal', but was not so flattering about the origins of the college:

> Queenwood College had been the Harmony Hall of the Socialists, which, under the auspices of the philanthropist, Robert Owen, was built to inaugurate the Millennium. The letters 'C and M', Commencement of Millennium, were actually inserted in flint in the brickwork of the house. Schemes like Harmony Hall look admirable upon paper; but inasmuch as they are formed with reference to an ideal humanity, they go to pieces when brought into collision with the real one.[77]

Also among the college's alumni was the local Henry Fawcett, a subsequent Member of Parliament and a defender of Charles Darwin's theories. Queenwood continued for a while after Edmondson's death, but slowly declined and served various purposes, including a poultry farm. In 1902 it burnt down and was completely destroyed by fire, at the same time causing the death of the previous head, who chose to remain there in residence. Every conceivable attempt was made to save him, but it was impossible to reach him, a heavy sleeper locked in a top-floor bedroom.[78] Any remains such as there were were sold and removed from the site. Only a small part of one of the kitchen walls remains.

---

76 *www.oxforddnb.com/articles/8/8489* – Edmondson.
77 *New Fragments,* John Tyndall, FRS, p.231 (New York, 1896).
78 *Salisbury and Winchester Journal, and General Advertiser,* 14 June 1902.

22. South London Rational School, 3 Blackfriars Road

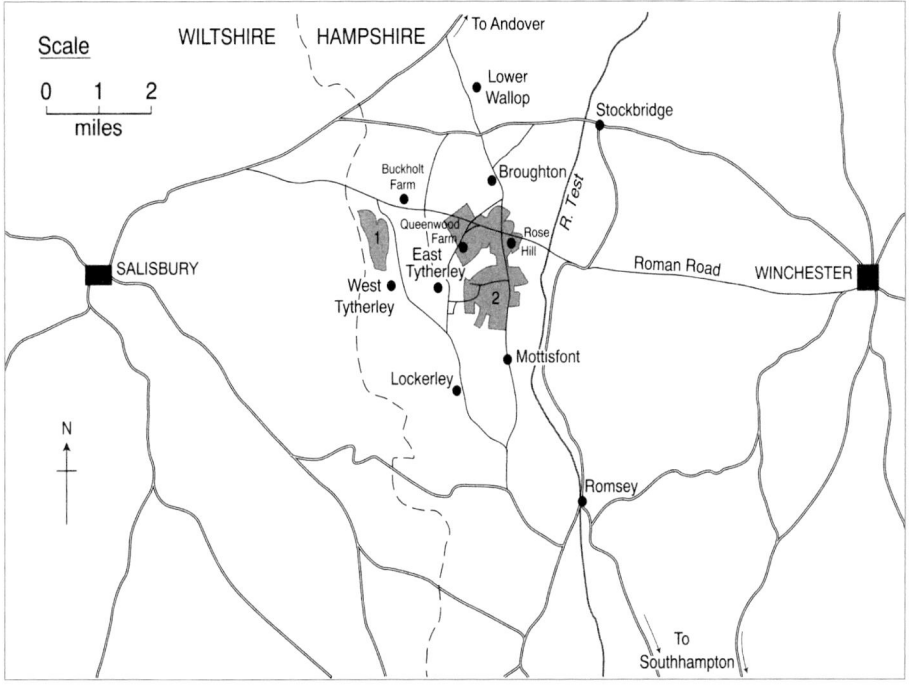

23. Location of the community in the parish of East Tytherley

Key
- Main roads
- Minor roads
- Country boundary
- River Test
- 1. Baring Wall's Norman Court
- 2. Harmony Community

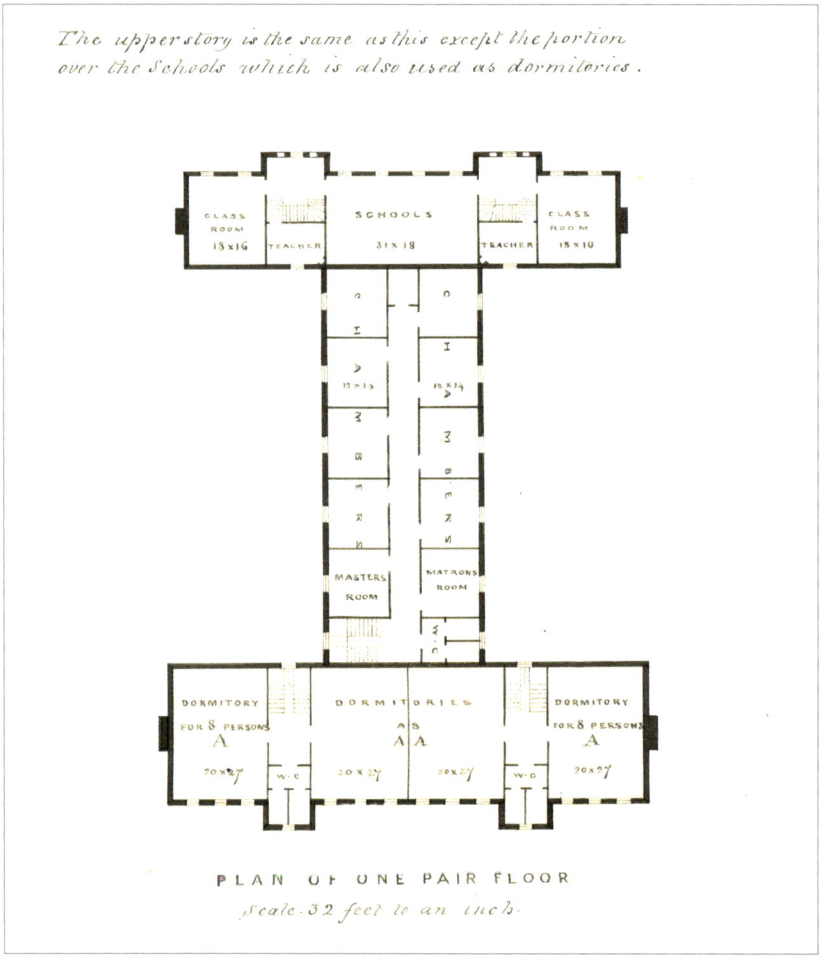

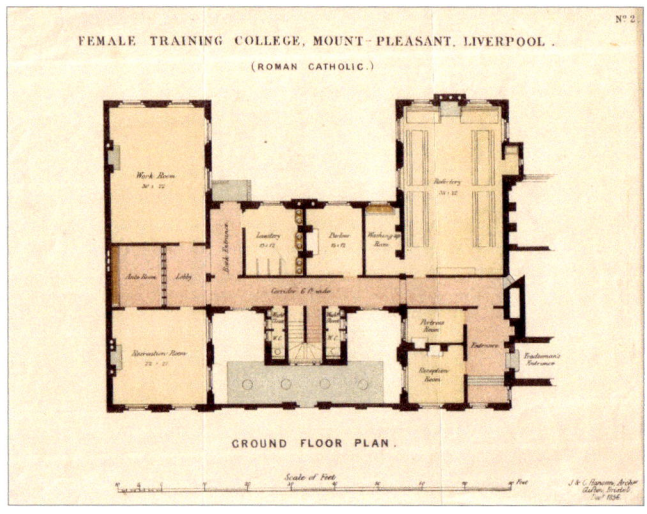

Comparison of Hansom's H-plans:

24(a). Above: Plan of one pair floor, Harmony Hall – Senate House Special Collection, William Pare Scrapbook, M.S. 578, 1839

24(b). Left: Training College for Catholic Schoolmistresses, Hansom 1857

25. *Harmony Hall (later Queenwood College) showing avenue of yews*

26. Tulketh Hall

27. Extant kitchen wall at Tytherley

CHAPTER V

THE AFTERMATH – *where next?*

OWEN

The theory put forward by Duncan, that Owen outlived his own career, is an interesting one.[1] He suggests that had Owen been content with his success at New Lanark, his reputation would have been very different. However this was unrealistic and not likely to happen. Owen was never satisfied and constantly frustrated that he could not convert more people, especially government, to assist in putting his theories into practice. His trip to America, the rise and fall of the Grand National Consolidated Trades Union and the demise of Harmony Hall confused and blurred his overall legacy. Furthermore Owen's benign and passive, yet stubbornly dictatorial approach, together with numerous financial irregularities, brought discord, not harmony. He had several long-term supporters, such as James Rigby and Lord Brougham; but his anti-religious views and his disagreements with Allen and Maclure stymied his chances of greater success. Delivering four papers to the Manchester Literary and Philosophical Society was indeed an achievement, but nothing to compare with the intellectual upbringings and sophisticated prowess of

---

1 Duncan, Floyd, H., *The Utopian Prince, Robert Owen and the Search for Millennium*, (revised edition, 2004).

the partners who became his successors. Owen knew all the right people and corresponded with aristocracy and influential politicians (often one and the same), and he received their hospitality on many occasions, but he was never accepted as one of them. The early death of the Duke of Kent in 1820, along with the support and the patronage he bestowed, was a great loss. Ironically, it was Allen who introduced the Duke of Kent to Owen.

As for his legacy, this is most commonly associated with New Lanark, the village or community which he superimposed upon a pre-existing industrial site. Originally comprising a cluster of four cotton mills, Mill number 4 had to be demolished due to heavy deterioration beyond repair, whilst the other three remained in production until 1968. The whole site was only saved from demolition by the New Lanark Conservation Trust. As in Owen's time, New Lanark is once again a well-known national showpiece, with the Reception area being called The Institute for the Formation of Character, named after one of his main themes. The complex provides a mix of heritage and memorabilia along with sensitive modernisation to allow for a hive of activity appropriate to its current usage. One of only six UNESCO World Heritage Sites in Scotland, its location is adjacent to land owned by the Scottish Wildlife Nature Trust, through which the River Clyde and its spectacular waterfall flow. They both receive a high volume of enthusiastic visitors, including many children.

Owen was responsible for taking the Pestalozzi system to America and the establishment became the first American public school for boys and girls, but his legacy at New Harmony rests largely with his sons Robert Dale and David. Owen never fully understood the American community. It either disintegrated or simply refused to adapt to his plans. It was left to his son and William Maclure to turn it into the success it became. It survived numerous upheavals and eventually flourished under a totally different banner. As Maclure's health gradually failed, the school was taken over by Mme Fretageot, Neef and the other French Pestalozzi teacher, Guillaume Phiquepal.

Described as one of Owen's most eccentric endeavours, Harmony Hall, or Queenwood, had no commercial foundation, nor was it ever likely to have.[2] It needed Owen's presence as a figurehead right from the start, a clear mission statement and a public 'voice', or newspaper; though, despite these deficiencies, it survived far longer than either Orbiston or its role model, Ralahine. However, the agricultural model of the latter did not fit in with the proposed location, neither were its inhabitants sufficiently numerous or skilled to run it. Thus, notwithstanding the 'CM' inscription, it failed dismally to bring forth Owen's apocalyptic concept of a millennium. After the collapse of Harmony Hall, Owen returned to America, where he spent

---

2 Davis and O'Hagan, *Robert Owen*, p.67.

three years with his family and still continued to lecture. However he was back in England again by 1847, living on a small annuity provided by his sons. He then embarked upon the building of social institutions called Halls of Science, but as his personal influence had fallen off, they made little impact.[3]

Very late in life, at the age of 85, Owen was still struggling on, and wrote five papers for the National Association for the Promotion of Social Science, formed in Birmingham in 1857. Lord Brougham was president for seven of its first nine years. Even at this late stage, Owen still had so much conviction in his beliefs that he started up the *Robert Owen Millennial Gazette,* which lasted until his death.[4] Brougham also supported Owen physically, when he firstly had to be lifted onto the platform in a sedan chair, and then helped down as he collapsed while delivering his last paper in Liverpool. It was not long after this that he returned to his home town of Newtown, to which he was accompanied by Rigby and his eldest son Robert Dale. He said that he wished to 'lay his bones from whence they had derived'. As Owen lay dying, he never faltered in the fanatical wisdom of 'his truth'. With murmurings of setting up yet more meetings, he faded away. His last words were 'Very easy and comfortable … relief has come'.[5] He had done all he could. Owing to his outspoken negative views on religion, he had considerable difficulty in persuading the local rector to permit his burial in St Mary's churchyard alongside his parents. However it was finally agreed. William Pare, his long-time supporter from Birmingham, attended the funeral. In 1902, with the help of the Co-operative Union, George Holyoake managed to enhance the original, simple grave stone. In his dedication ceremony Holyoake eulogised:

> 'thanks to the doctrine of national environment which Owen was the first to preach, knowledge is greater, life is longer, health is surer, disease is limited, towns are sweeter, hours of labour are shorter, men are stronger, women are fairer, and children are happier.'

The ornate iron railing now placed around the grave consists of foliage designs and neo-classical symbols, with a portrait of Owen surrounded by workmen as the centrepiece. A grand memorial to Owen was erected in Kensal Green Cemetery, where John Gibson and Henry Fawcett were buried, as were Isambard Brunel, Anthony Trollope and many well-known nineteenth century personalities. Perhaps, after death, Owen was finally accepted amongst national heroes. Coincidentally, 1902 was the year in which Queenwood College burnt to the ground.

---

3 Floyd, *Utopian Prince*, pp.356-357.
4 McCabe, *Robert Owen*, p.117.
5 Podmore, *biography,* p.629.

Children

After Owen left America, New Harmony became the extended family home of his sons.[6] Like Maclure, they became American citizens. Robert Dale, Owen's eldest son was a Congressman and author. He was a United States Representative between 1843 and 1847, and Minister Resident to the Two Sicilies between 1853 and 1858. He was not the first to admit that his father was incorrect in thinking that some of his ideas were entirely original.[7] William, a merchant and banker, died comparatively young, at the age of forty.[8] When debts at New Harmony had previously mounted up to an unacceptable level, he had been saved from gaol by his brother Robert Dale who borrowed £2,000 on his own security.[9] Their younger bother, David Dale, specialised in geology and led surveys of Arkansas, Indian and Kentucky. He was married to Caroline Neef, daughter of the Pestalozzi teacher Joseph Neef, and became a prime instigator of the Smithsonian Institute, a group of museums and research centres aiming to increase and diffuse scientific knowledge.

HANSOM

Hansom's later life was certainly not hazard-free. There were arguments as to the future management of his Hansom Cab Company, and though he was offered the sum of £10,000, all he ever received was £300, a fee to sort out the financial muddle created by his successors. Had he received the £10,000 this would have been life-changing. His college would have been able to develop and grow into the success it deserved and Hansom might also have been able to retain his editorship of *The Builder*. However, he had to fall back on his core profession as a source of income. This did not leave him short of work. He had the support of the Jesuits and was in great demand. He erected thirteen schools between 1845 and 1856 alone, in addition to numerous churches and a wide variety of other buildings across the country, from the conversion of a fort built in 1729 into a Benedictine Monastery in Scotland; to a complex of cathedral, Bishop's House and convent in Devon; down to the building of Arundel Cathedral for the Duke of Norfolk. Plymouth Cathedral, the spire of which replicated that of his St Walburge's church in Preston (still the tallest church spire in the country), caused havoc when part of the building collapsed during construction. A police cordon was called in to protect it. The builder blamed the architect and the architect blamed the builder.[10] On another occasion, Hansom was erecting a small church in Scotland and the American benefactor declined to pay tonnage for the very

---

6 Pollard, *Prophet*, p.226.
7 Cole, *Robert Owen*, p.74.
8 Pollard, *Prophet*, p.226.
9 Royle, *millennium*, p.19.
10 *The Builder*, 13 June 1857, p.342.

large ship which had delivered stone from the South of England. The ship blocked the entrance to a tiny harbour as the captain demanded payment. Hansom had to beg a loan from an ecclesiastical colleague, and then pay the balance himself. Both humiliating and embarrassing, but not a problem of his making.

In addition to these, Hansom designed several convents and a theologate in Wales. They were mainly built to be self-sufficient and emulated Owen's concept of communities. The most notable were St Mary's in Leeds, and the Welsh college at St Asaph. Had Hansom had the opportunity to complete Leeds, it would have been one of his most extensive. However, due to shortage of funds, it was built in stages, and finally completed by William Wardell. The site was on the top of a hill which turned out to be unstable due to old mine shafts underneath. It comprised a church, a school, a convent and an orphanage, more-or-less amounting to a village – certainly worthy of the term 'community'. St Beuno's, the College in Wales, had its own water supply, generated its own gas and had a unique solar system run through pipes from large greenhouses into the main building. Being on a steeply sloping site, the land was terraced to enable vegetables to be grown. Mainly restricted to adult males, it was a place of education and another self-contained community which additionally ran a small school for local children. Regrettably, both St Walburge and St Mary have been listed in the Victorian Society's Top Ten Most Endangered Buildings. St Walburge thrives as a going concern under new ownership, but St Mary's is near derelict. St Beuno's flourishes, though in a slightly different way.

Clear in mind until the end, but like Owen, still abounding with ideas, Hansom was crippled with arthritis for the last two and a half years of his life. During this time he devoted himself to preparing for his final moment. He died peacefully at his London home in the Fulham Road, London, surrounded by his family. Buried alongside his wife, his gravestone is a small, humble one in a nearby churchyard.[11] Regrettably the carved symbols are fading away, and his inscription is hidden by earth.

Children

Hansom's eldest son was also a talented architect, briefly in partnership with his father. However, his track-record is somewhat overshadowed by arguments with Battersea Council, where he was District Surveyor. The arrangement was that Henry John should also be permitted to carry out his own work, but apparently he exceeded his limitations. One of his best known works is the church and priest house of St Joseph, East Greenwich.[12] Joseph

---

11 Herbert Gribble, Hansom's pupil who designed the Brompton Oratory, and three of Dickens' infant great-grandchildren are buried in the same cemetery.
12 See *Victorian Web*.

Stanislaus, Hansom's youngest son also partnered his father and contributed to many of his larger, later works, one notable achievement being the Church of the Holy Name in Manchester. He had an interest in history and founded of the *Catholic Record Society*.

Birmingham too played its part and on-going links to Hansom's short-lived residency can be traced over many years. The Town Hall was closed in 1996 and its future was in doubt due to concerns as to its structural integrity. However, thanks to a massive donation from the Lottery Heritage Fund, it was extensively refurbished. It now continues to take a prominent part in Birmingham's programme of high-profile musical events, with a small area known as the Hansom Suite used for private functions. The building still stands strong, but is at the edge of the all-pervading Paradise Development which looms above it. Notwithstanding his financial losses, Hansom trained two renowned architects whilst in Birmingham, his younger brother Charles Francis, and the talented young pupil John Gibson. There was an age gap of fourteen years between Joseph and Charles as their middle brother died whilst they were in Birmingham. The effect which the Town Hall had on Charles was profound. He never forgave his father for the financial muddle which ensued, and declared that he would 'never build a town hall'. He turned for solace to a local priest, William Ullathorne, who was also a Yorkshire-man and was to become the first Bishop of Birmingham. Not being in a position to extend Charles' training further, Ullathorne took Charles to Belgium, Germany and France 'to educate his taste and stimulate his ideas'.[13] Ullathorne took a genuine interest in the development of Gothic architecture and this contact provided Charles with much work.

Gibson was fortunate in being able to complete his training with Charles Barry in London. Amongst his most prestigious works was his Baptist Chapel in Bloomsbury, contiguous with Hansom's Baptist Chapel in Leicester; but above all the Hansom/Birmingham influence is most clearly seen in Todmorden on the Lancashire/Yorkshire border. Here, in 1866, Gibson designed a town hall for the Fielden family. John Fielden, a long-time campaigner for shorter working hours, was a Radical textile manufacturer and owner of a large cotton-spinning business. At the time of the fourth congress in 1832, when membership of the Birmingham Co-operative Society was beginning to drop off, it was steadily increasing in Todmorden. They had 250 members, compared with only twenty-nine in Birmingham.[14] The following year, in Manchester, Owen had formed a Society for National Regeneration together with Fielden, William Cobbett and John Doherty.[15] Both Fielden and Cobbett became Members of Parliament for Oldham. As Gibson would

---
13 Champ, Judith, *William Bernard Ullathorne: A Different Kind of Monk*, p.116.
14 Garnett, *Co-operation*, p.139.
15 Cole, *Robert Owen*, p.195.

undoubtedly have worked on the Town Hall in Birmingham, it is easy to see how this influenced his choice of design in Tordmorden. His hall was on an island site, in classical style, with columns and carved capitals similar to those in Birmingham. It is not quite as tall as its archetype, and the auditorium only holds 250 people, but nevertheless it is a very imposing building. Being privately funded, Gibson was able to embellish it with detailed carving. Like Hansom's Lutterworth Town Hall, it has one curved end.

EPILOGUE

This book is seemingly about people, their aspirations and their interactions, their working and living conditions; but it is also about the power of architecture. The names of architects are often forgotten or overlooked, yet the significance of their buildings is paramount and repeatedly depicted in the press of the time as 'ornaments to the town'. Buildings are historical palimpsests as much as any words or deeds, and should be acknowledged as such.

Owen and Hansom were two very different men. They had much in common, but totally different ways of projecting their views on the world around them. They were both philanthropists with strong moral ideals. Both were popular with many devoted followers, however differences appear in their approach. Owen, the self-styled prophet and quasi religious guru who denied religion, had such a complex personality that it confounds analysis. He was called a tyrant and a dictator; but also a lover of little children, the 'Socialist father' and a potential new patron saint of Wales. On the other hand, should he need to describe himself, Hansom called himself 'the architect of Birmingham Town Hall', whereas general descriptions, such as those of his churches, identify him as 'the designer of the hansom cab'. Joseph Stanislaus described his father simply as:

> A man of strong ideas and strong ideals, he was not a seeker of fame or fortune, but quite prepared to defend his own abilities when the need arose. To his clients and pupils under him he was full of kindness, a character of much power mingled with still greater gentleness.[16]

One of the main differences between them was that Owen was inflexible, stuck rigidly to his theories and repeated them *ad nauseam*, unlike Hansom who was willing to listen to others and adapt to circumstances. On sifting through the morass of Owen's repetition, many statements of sound common sense can be found, along with a few futuristic gems, such as his allusion to railways being nationalised and the idea of travel by air. However,

---

16 *The Builder*, 8 July 1883.

others are so extreme that they were not remotely plausible, like the question of the GNCTU becoming the 'House of Trades' and replacing the House of Commons; removing mountains to flatten the world, and insisting upon 'nothing but the very best' at Tytherley, when the community was already sinking under debt.[17]

As an individual, Owen was almost forgotten by the end of the nineteenth century. However, because education was so important to him, it could be argued that he did indeed achieve his ambition, for both New Harmony and Queenwood College became prestigious and highly successful educational establishments, albeit after he had left and not in the communitarian or millennial way which he intended. His legacy also remains in the on-going Co-operative movement, high street stores and pre-school nurseries, though none bear his name. Added to these must also be his success in triggering factory reform and reducing working hours. He was also a major contributor to the burgeoning Socialist party. Thus, on balance the list is impressive. However, an eternal optimist, he relied too heavily on rich donors, and the sale of surplus goods which never materialised. He could aptly be likened to an 'absentee landlord', and therein lay much of his downfall. He travelled too much, evangelising rather than pursuing his schemes at a day-to-day level, unlike Hansom who was in constant touch by letter even when time and distance precluded site visits. Owen's self-description as a 'practical' person is questionable.[18] Were not Hansom's little church schools of more practical use than Owen's unrealisable theories? Both New Lanark and New Harmony were, after all, already thriving commercially when he took over. Harmony Hall was a forlorn hope – the culmination of all his ideas and experiences, cobbled together with no infrastructure, no financial backing and in quite the wrong location.

Owen's 'happiness' was also only ever a pipe dream – the glimmer of a smile is rarely to be seen in any of his many portraits. His condemnation of religion in the London Tavern was a case of 'self destruct'. That he repeated it in America beggars belief. Owen never fully grew up. His childhood ideas transmuted into large-scale management and then social reform, but they never developed fully, becoming like a record, stuck in a groove. More than anything else, it was his religious views which led to the break-up of his first two communities. Whilst Edmondson founded his establishment at Tytherley on Hofwyl lines and promoted the formation of character, he also made it clear in his synopsis of the course that this was only valuable when 'based on Christian principles … either of the Established church or through Dissenting chapels'.[19]

---
17 Morton, L., *The life and ideas of Robert Owen,* (London, 1962), p.54.
18 Royle, *millennium,* p.12.
19 Prospectus, Queenwood College, *Hampshire Record Office,* 47M66/12/1.

Owen's Birmingham phase was a short, sharp, self-contained period of his life, and though he returned on many occasions, it had little relevance to his future. He seemed oblivious as to the consequences of his actions on others. Hansom's life was temporarily overturned, and, of course, it effectively brought Welch's career to a premature end. However, Hansom's career had barely begun. Like Owen, he was a man of ideas. An eclectic rather than a radical, he was by no means void of imagination or easily swayed by convention. Long after his time in Birmingham, Evinson describes his design approach variously as perverse with rebellious touches of defiance.[20] His originality showed up in his architectural designs, such as those for the memorials of the Duke of Sussex and Nelson, neither of which was selected.

Above all, Hansom should be remembered for his *Builder* (or *Building*), which continues to commemorate its founder, the Town Hall and his eponymous cab, the one perpetuated by its world-class concerts and the other by its association with Sherlock Holmes. When comparing their funeral monuments, Owen's now-enhanced grave-stone in Newtown and his elaborate memorial in Kensal Green Cemetery, with Hansom's humble gravestone in London, these are not indicators of success. They are more a reflection of their differing personalities. If either of them is to have the last word as to fame, then it might yet rest with Owen. Plans were mooted for the building of Owenstown, 3,200 houses to be built on a 21,000 acre site a few miles from New Lanark. It was proposed that the town would be self-managed on 'co-operative' principles, energy efficient and with low carbon emissions, and comprising houses, schools, a factory and all the usual facilities expected of a modern town. Unsurprisingly, the original application was rejected mainly on the grounds that the land was 'unsuitable for agriculture' and 'lack of interest', (ie manpower) – a repeat of Harmony Hall, without the manor house. Plans are in abeyance and Owen's Utopia is, therefore, still awaited.

---

20 Evinson, pp.50, 213.

The Aftermath – where next?

28(a). Gravestone of Robert Owen

28(b). Gravestone of Joseph Hansom

29. Remains of St Mary's Church, Leeds

30(a). St Walburge's Church, Preston

30(b). St Mary and St Boniface Cathedral church, Plymouth

31(a). St Beuno's College, showing terracing

31(b). St Beuno's College, showing greenhouse

32. Todmorden Town Hall

33. *Hansom cab rank in Colmore Row*

APPENDIX I

TIME LINE

ROBERT OWEN 1771-1858   **JOSEPH HANSOM 1803-1882**

1800	managing partner of New Lanark	
1813	purchased New Lanark	
1818	European journey	
1822	first visit to Ireland	
1825	purchased New Harmony	
1825-26	December-January: Boatload of Knowledge	
1827-29		York Dispensary (demolished)
1828	left New Harmony	1828-35: working in Yorkshire, Liverpool and Anglesey
	(November: Pare founded Birmingham Co-operative Society)	
1830	Birmingham Labour Exchange Gazette	December: BTH competition advertised
	(Birmingham Political Union founded)	
1831	2nd Congress in Birmingham May: Ralahine set up	February: closing date for competition June: Hansom & Welch appointed
1832	National Equitable Exchanges *The Crisis,* April 1832	BTH foundation stone laid
	(May: New Hall Hill Meeting, BPU/Attwood)	
	(June: Great Reform Bill)	

1833	September: Grand Meeting, Manchester (Owen/Hansom/Welch) end of Ralahine (Ireland) September: former journal of the Builders' Union became *The Pioneer*	August: aborted attempt to build Grammar School November: work started on Operative Builders' Guildhall
	(Factories Act)	
1834	February: Grand National Consolidated Trades Union formed November: *NMW* founded	February: work ceased on Guildhall April: declared bankrupt June: Guildhall re-started briefly, then finally ceased December: patented hansom cab
	(18 March: start of Tolpuddle Martyrs trial) (25 April: Derby lockout)	
1835	Association of All Classes of All Nations founded	designed Lutterworth Town Hall
	(Prisons Act)	
1836	First Annual Congress, London	Leicester Proprietary School
1837		Bulkeley Arms Hotel, Beaumaris Rosary Convent, Atherstone St Mary's Priory, Princethorpe
1838	*NMW* moved to Birmingham October: Special Congress, Birmingham	Hinckley Union Workhouse
1839	May: 4th Annual Congress, Birmingham October: purchased Queenwood Farm	
1840	plans for new building outlined	
1841	*New Moral World* ceased August: RO laid foundation stone	Moved to London Building work for HH commenced

1842	Move from Queenwood to HH 7th Annual Congress at HH May: RO appointed Governor July: Galpin acting Governor August: Pare deputy Governor October: Secondary school opened	reorganisation of Tulketh Hall modified Mount St Mary's College, Spinkhill, Derbyshire December: precursor issue *The Builder*
1843	Elementary school opened 8th Annual Congress, at HH Owen re-appointed Governor	
1844	9th Annual Congress, at HH	
1845	10th Annual Congress, at HH *NMW* moved to HH September: closed due to financial crisis	
1846	Harmony Estate Protection Committee Smithsonian Institute	Foundation stone St Walburge church
1847	HH leased to Geo Edmondson, Pare, J.Finch, E.Finch & Davis Queenwood College opened with Edmondson as Principal	

notes: BTH = Birmingham Town Hall; HH = Harmony Hall; NMW = New Moral World
only a selection of Hansom's main works is listed

APPENDIX II

SHORT BIOGRAPHIES

Academics at Queenwood College

Queenwood College flourished under Edmondson's leadership. Amongst its teachers were, Heinrich Debus, a German chemist who taught at Queenwood between 1851 and 1868. After that he became Senior Master at Clifton Catholic College Bristol (designed by Hansom's brother Charles), taught at Guy's Hospital and became Professor of Chemistry at the Royal Naval College, Greenwich. Sir Edward Frankland, a research chemist from Lancashire, was science master at Queenwood in 1847, before moving to Germany, then back to England to become a professor at what is now Manchester University. John Tyndall was an Irish physicist and mathematician with expertise in surveying and advising railway companies.[1] All three studied under Robert Wilhelm Bunsen. A notable alumnus was Henry Fawcett, born in Salisbury, who went on to King's College, Cambridge and became a barrister. He then became Professor of Political Economy at Cambridge and postmaster-general under Gladstone.[2] Though blinded in a shooting incident, he was still able to become a Member of Parliament.

William Allen, 1770-1843

An upbringing based on Quaker principles dominated Allen's life from an early age. His father was a silk manufacturer in whose business he worked before developing an interest in the sciences and transferring to a career in pharmacy. His Quaker connections led him to give up sugar in protest of the slave trade. Wilberforce represented the abolitionists in the House of Parliament as, being a Quaker, Allen was not allowed to stand. He was, however, a member

34. William Allen

---

1 In 1863 Tyndall's research led him to be described as 'the first climate change believer'; Baum, *https://sciencehistory.org/distillations/magazine/future-calculations*, **2** (2) (38-39).
2 Royle, *millennium*, p.211.

of the committee which represented the Society for the Abolition of the Slave Trade. Allen was an educationalist with an interest in nutrition and self-sufficient communities, having set up a model agricultural settlement at Lindfield. He suggested that instead of encouraging emigration, groups should be persuaded to set up 'Colonies at Home'. In 1824 he founded the Quaker Newington College for Girls in 1824, at which he also taught. As for his pharmaceutical career, he achieved Fellowship of the Royal Society in 1807, became President of the Physical Society at Guy's Hospital, where he lectured, and co-founded The Pharmaceutical Society in 1841. His pharmaceutical company went into partnership with Daniel Hanbury, a relative of his second wife, and subsequently became the well-known pharmaceutical firm of Allen and Hanbury. Though taken over by GlaxoSmithKline, their name was still used until 2013.

He was a personal friend of Jeremy Bentham, hence Bentham's involvement with New Lanark. The combination of Allen's various interests, his past experience and the contacts he gained during his extensive travels on the Continent between 1818 and 1820, demonstrate clearly why New Lanark had appeal. However he became increasingly offended by Owen's stance on religion, particularly when Owen suggested to Allen that instead of reading the Bible pupils would derive 'more real benefit' from learning geography.[3] Owen's dismissal was determined at a management meeting in London, when it was suggested that Owen's three shares be purchased. Owen managed to circumvent this by transferring one share to each of his sons.

Thomas Attwood, 1765-1856

Attwood's contribution to the passing of the Great Reform Bill is seen by some to be exaggerated, becoming a myth unique to Birmingham and Attwood historians. Described as 'undistinguished in appearance, with an angular face, wiry hair, dark complexion and somber eyes' he was easily recognised by his symbolic wearing of a coat with a fur collar at any time of the year.[4] A local man, born in Halesowen, Shropshire, and eighteen years older than Hansom, he came from a wealthy family which supported the industrial revolution. His grandfather had extensive iron, copper and steel interests. His father used the profits from his iron trade to open a bank in London, followed by a branch in New Street, Birmingham. Charles, one of his younger brothers and an active member of

35. *Thomas Attwood – portrait by W. Green*

---

3 Donnachie, *Owen of New Lanark,* p.197.
4 Flick, *BPU,* p.19.

the Newcastle Political Union, was an ironmaster in Newcastle, where he patented a new method of steelmaking.

Attwood joined the Birmingham branch in 1799. In 1812 he led a successful move to revoke an embargo on trade with America, which was threatening trade and worsening unemployment. At this point he distrusted political reform *per se,* but became interested in universal suffrage and was concerned at the lack of representation for growing towns such as Birmingham and Manchester. He also started to campaign for currency reform, believing that abundant bank notes would solve society's problems, and, in Owen-like terms, spoke of 'saving the country'. Encouraged by O'Connell's success with the Catholic Association in getting Roman Catholic emancipation, Attwood started to organise 'monster' meetings such as O'Connell's. The BPU was launched in 1830 with just 6,000 members, and eventually it became so successful that Attwood was described as 'the most influential man in England'.[5] Cobbett was shortly to call him 'King Tom'. It was at this stage that the ideas of 'common interests of employers and employees' (see Hansom's article in *The Builder*), and 'masters and men being one and the same' came into being. During 1831 and 1832 Attwood held regular open-air meetings of between 50,000 and 200,000 people. His first attempt to pass the Great Reform Bill was rejected in November 1831. A revised bill was passed in the Commons in May 1832, though Attwood was not satisfied and said he would 'rather die than see the great bill of reform rejected or mutilated'.[6] Grey's resignation prevented it from reaching the Lords, and Attwood uncharacteristically considered forming a national guard, which led to rumours that he (and Hansom) might be arrested. When Wellington also resigned, the bill was finally passed through the Lords in June 1832. By then the loss of support from the working-classes precipitated the closure of the BPU.

Disillusionment set in. The bill had in fact been mutilated and his currency theories were rejected. He did, however, achieve incorporation for Birmingham in 1837, and he and Scholefield became Birmingham's first Members of Parliament. Two years later, rioting broke out in Birmingham and Attwood's attempt to join with the Chartist movement was a failure. It became apparent that Attwood was more suited to Birmingham than Westminster, and with his health beginning to fail, he resigned in 1839. He moved to Harborne, four miles from Birmingham, but when he decided to dispose of the family bank, he discovered that his brother, who had been running it for him, had fallen into heavy debt. He finally moved to Great Malvern, where he died in very straightened circumstances and suffering from Parkinson's disease.[7]

---
5 Brock, M., *The Great Reform Act* (London, 1974) p.62.
6 Wakefield, C.M., *Life of Thomas Attwood* (London, 1885), pp.207, 209.
7 *ODNB*, on-line version, accessed 22 September 2019.

Henry Peter, Lord Brougham, 1778-1868

Like many other loyal Owen supporters, the name of Henry Peter Brougham appears frequently throughout Owen's campaigns, from the time of his London Tavern speeches, through till his final effort in Liverpool. Brougham was a Whig MP and a key contact between Birmingham and London during the attempts to bring about Attwood's Reform Bill, and the Slavery Abolition Act which passed the following year.[8] Brougham's interest in education was first demonstrated in 1816, when he presided over the Committee for the Education of the Lower Orders in the Metropolis, and concluded that 'a very large number of children are wholly without the means of instruction...'.[9] He had previously been a Member of Parliament for Hansom's home county, Yorkshire, in 1830, and held the position of Lord High Chancellor until 1834. He poached one of Owen's teachers from New Lanark and attempted to set up a school in London, but it failed due to James Buchanan, the teacher, diverting from Owen's methodology. Coincidentally the Brougham, a four-wheeler horse-drawn carriage was named after him. Hansom considered that his cab was safer, being less likely to tip over while being driven.

John Doherty, 1798-1854

Of Irish descent, Doherty worked as a cotton spinner up to the age of ten. His family moved to Belfast, and then Manchester in 1816. By 1818 he had become a leading figure in the Amalgamated Association of Operative Cotton Spinners and leader of the Manchester Spinners Union. He tried to link English spinners unions with those in Ireland and Scotland, but they refused to join. When the spinners' strike collapsed, he was imprisoned for two years. On his release he became a bookseller and printer, publishing the radical journal entitled *The Voice of the People*. Doherty was also instrumental in campaigning for the reduction of working hours, leading to the Ten Hours Bill and the 1847 Factory Acts.

George Edmondson, 1798-1863

Born in Lancaster of Quaker parents, Edmondson left school with aspirations to become a teacher. He trained with a bookbinder, who also gave him a grounding in agriculture. As tutor to his mentor's children, Edmondson moved to Russia, where they both lived until 1820. After a brief spell in England, he returned to Russia to assist in bringing bog land back into cultivation. Having rejected an offer from Alexander I to remain in Russia, he returned once again to England, where he set up a school in Blackburn. Ambition led him to expand and he purchased Tulketh Hall, near Preston.

---

8 The sister of Attwood's partner, Spooner, was married to William Wilberforce.
9 Podmore, *biography*, p.103.

Though not yet personally involved with Harmony Hall, Edmondson would have been aware of Hansom's reputation as an architect, and accordingly commissioned him to convert his newly acquired Hall for use as a school. The school quickly became so successful that it was turning away pupils. However, as the financial difficulties and personality clashes at Queenwood became public knowledge, and Owen was forced out, Edmondson relinquished Tulketh Hall and entered into a 99-year lease at £600 *per annum,* renaming the former community Queenwood College. This was in June 1847, exactly one year after the Buxton family, John being the President of the flagging Rational Society and last Governor of Harmony Hall, had been physically ejected from the premises and left at the roadside overnight.[10]

Within the first twelve months of Edmondson taking over, he invested £1000 of his own money on making improvements. Like Owen and Pestalozzi, Edmondson believed in 'practical' teaching, and included two teachers from Hofwyl amongst his staff. He raised the level of education in similar manner to that at New Harmony, and Queenwood was shortly to be recognised as having 'the most impressive list of future scientists in any [British] scholastic establishment during the nineteenth-century'. Edmondson's interest in education was such that he became a founder member of the College of Preceptors, set up to regulate the burgeoning teaching profession. However, he also inherited a legacy which left a trail of numerous bankruptcy claims and lengthy Chancery proceedings led by Pare. The College fell into decline following litigation between Edmondson and the trustees, mainly with regard to the terms of the lease. It was not until 1863 that a final decree was determined, the stress from which may have led to Edmondson's sudden death.

Marie Duclos Fretageot, 1783-1832
Marie Fretageot was a close friend of Maclure. She had already established a school in Paris based on Pestalozzi principles, and it was she who encouraged Maclure to participate in Owen's communitarian philosophy in Indiana.[11] On her way to Indiana she wrote to Maclure expressing her delight at having met Owen and saying that his principles were so much in harmony with her own.[12] She described a talk by him as 'the best man explaining a plan which is best calculated for human happiness'.[13] For a more in-depth analysis, see Bestor, Arthur Eugene, 'Education and Reform at New Harmony: Correspondence of William Maclure and Marie Duclos Fretageot', *Historical Society,* 'Publications', vol.XV, no.3, 1948.

---

10 Garnett, pp.214-215.
11 Donnachie, *Owen of New Lanark,* p.216.
12 Cole, *Robert Owen,* p.148.
13 Donnachie, *ibid.,* p.217.

John Galpin, 1802-1849

One of Owen's most loyal supporters and a peace-maker, Galpin was six foot tall with whitish-grey hair, a black beard and dark piercing eyes.[14] He was the first chairman of the Wiltshire and Dorset Bank. When a former General Secretary of the Owenite Rational Society, he complained to Owen via the *New Moral World,* that he regretted Owen not living at Queenwood, 'to impart his knowledge of what was most needed'.[15] Galpin made large personal donations and helped raise money by means of a joint stock company. However, his insistence upon the use of only the best building materials led to accusations of his having encouraged excessive expenditure. He left in 1843, stating that 'It is enough for me that there existed a feeling that the cause might be better served by my ceasing to be one of its officers'.[16] He ultimately set up a small colony on the Bentley estate, where previous members of Harmony Hall attempted to live a spartan vegetarian life. This only lasted for a short time, as they were beleaguered with on-going problems concerning the lease. Emma Pare, daughter of William Pare, married Galpin's son, Thomas Dixon.[17]

George Holyoake, 1817-1906

A true Brummagem, Holyoake's parents were a printer and a button-maker. His view of Birmingham was that it was 'precisely that kind of town where Co-operation should succeed'. An enthusiastic missionary, he was a passionate supporter of Owen, right through till after his death, when, as already stated, he was instrumental in enhancing Owen's gravestone. The building of Holyoake House, the Co-operative Headquarters in Manchester, commemorates his name. A self-proclaimed agitator

36. *George Holyoake*

and champion of the working classes, Holyoake is notable in that, whilst giving a lecture, he was tricked into answering a question about his views on religion. His response, 'I am of no religion at all ...', led directly to his prosecution for blasphemy, and a six-month gaol sentence in 1842.[18] Neutral rather than hostile to religion, this led to the term 'Secularism'.[19] Holyoake was nearly gaoled for a second time when he published an unstamped newspaper, another of his campaigns.

---

14 Royle, *millennium,* p.133, quoting *NMW,* 13 September 1845.
15 Brown, W. Henry, *Pathfinders* (Manchester, 1997), p.12.
16 Brown, *ibid.*
17 Garnett, *Co-operation,* p.219.
18 Podmore, *biography,* p.527.
19 Gilley, Sheridan, 'Industrialization, Empire, Identity', in Gilley, Sheridan and Shiels, W.J. (eds.), *A History of Religion in Britain: practice and belief from pre-Roman times to the present* (Oxford, 1994), p.412.

Like Owen, he was a prolific writer and the report of his visit to Harmony Hall is one of the most colourful and the most detailed. His attempts to keep the Rational Society alive continued until it broke up in 1845, after which he became editor of the *Reasoner*, which continued until 1861.[20] The weekly periodical was described as 'Communisitic in Social Economy, Utilitarian in Morals, Republican in Politics, and Anti-theological in Religion'. Amongst other writings, Holyoake also authored the *Life and Last Days of Robert Owen* in 1859 and *The History of Co-operation,* from 1875.

William Maclure, 1763-1840

A scientist turned educational reformer, Maclure was the first to introduce Pestalozzian methods to the United States. The combination of a substantial inheritance and a successful business career had enabled him to retire early and devote his time to scholarship. He travelled extensively, especially in Ireland and France, where, having witnessed the French Revolution first hand, he gathered together a collection of 25,000 French Revolutionary pamphlets and literature. He had already turned his back on his home-land and when he moved permanently to Philadelphia in 1796, he became an American citizen. His interests were mainly mineralogy and geology and he became President of the Academy of National Science in Philadelphia 1817-1840, being appointed the first President of the American Geological Society 1819. However, like Owen, he was also interested in education for all, anti-slavery and women's rights. He was a patron of Pestalozzi, who he first visited in 1804, and financed both Neef's Pestlozzi school in Paris and that of Marie Fretageot.[21] Neef had already visited New Lanark in 1824, and was persuaded by Maclure to move to America.

37. *William Maclure*

Rev Thomas M McDonnell, 1792-1869

Born in East Grinstead, McDonnell was placed under the wing of the father of Bishop Mostyn when his father died. At ten years of age he was sent to the prestigious Catholic School at Sedgely Park in Staffordshire. Whilst here, and coinciding with the French Revolution, pupils staged many mock battles, with McDonnell a formidable opponent, being tall and of stocky build, something which stood him in good stead during his Birmingham campaigns. After

38. *Thomas McDonnell*

---
20 Podmore, *biography,* p.581.
21 Harrison, *Owenites in Britain,* p.220.

a spell at Oscott, he worked for the Earl of Surrey in Nottinghamshire, but he found the post too restrictive. His subsequent transfer to Birmingham 'seemed to unleash a great outpouring of energy'.[22] He became the parish priest of St Peter's Catholic Church in Broad Street, where he added side galleries, built a presbytery, purchased land for a Catholic burial ground and founded an orphanage. Despite giving much of his own money, these undertakings loaded him with debt, which was paid off by Pugin's Catholic benefactor, the Earl of Shrewsbury. He worked very long hours, preaching and supervising three schools, in addition to all the usual duties of a priest. However, like Hansom, he was caught up in the political and social changes taking place. A man of great determination, he founded the *Catholic Magazine,* to which Daniel O'Connell contributed. O'Connell stayed with him during his visits to Birmingham, but even though the BPU used the Irish Catholic Association as a role model, the connection between the two men was not welcome and they refused to pay O'Connell's expenses.[23]

McDonnell was immensely popular with his congregation, which he increased three-fold, but his political activities, together with the fact that he used the *Catholic Magazine* to voice his personal views and was instrumental in breaking down barriers between Catholics and Protestants, caused friction with the Catholic authorities. His final demise came about when the Earl, along with Pugin, suggested building a completely new Catholic Cathedral. McDonnell protested loudly in the belief that his own church, St Peter's, would be completely sidelined. Having lost this particular battle, the affray was the ultimate cause of his departure from Birmingham. His character softened later in life, when he retreated to the Western District and became Canon Theologian of the Goodridge pro-Cathedral at Clifton which Charles Hansom completed in 1848.[24]

Joseph Moore, 1766-1851

Educated at Worcester, Moore was sent to Birmingham in 1781 to learn die-sinking, after which he went into partnership in the button trade. In 1808 he founded the Birmingham Oratorio Choral Society to bring together local singers engaged in the Triennial Festivals. He did much to raise the profile of both the Hall and the Festivals across Europe and was responsible for encouraging Mendelssohn to compose the oratorio 'St Paul'. This was performed at the 1837 festival in Birmingham, and led to the first performance of 'Elija' in 1851.

---

22 Dennis O'Connor, 'Thomas McDonnell: A 19th Century Pastor of St Peter's Gloucester', *Gloucestershire Catholic History Society Journal* 32, 1997, p.29.
23 Flick, *BPU*, p.102.
24 Champ, 'Assimilation', p.184.

Daniel O'Connell, 1775-1847

39. Daniel O'Connell

The descendent of an Elizabethan settler in Ireland, O'Connell was born into a wealthy Catholic family in Co. Kerry which became dispossessed of its lands. He was a tall man, with fine, blue eyes, delicate hands, a strong musical voice and immense physical vigour.[25] In 1794 he inherited an estate from his uncle, and at an early age he was sent to The English College, a seminary in Douai which was subsequently suppressed during the French Revolution. Many English priests were executed, O'Connell was able to escape and trained as a lawyer at Lincoln's Inn. From there he moved to Dublin's King's Inns where he was finally admitted as a barrister in 1794. Strongly opposed to violence, he was caught in a personal dilemma between the fear of French invasion, an Irish rebellion and enlisting in the British army which was opposed to Catholicism. Aware that the general population was repressed in favour of a privileged minority, he became a champion of equal rights and strove to achieve Catholic Emancipation. He urged tenants to vote only for candidates who were in favour of Emancipation.[26] O'Connell's connection with Owen and Hansom was more on the political front, through Attwood and McDonnell, though his Catholic Association, and especially his 'monster' meetings were mirrored by Owen throughout his life.

William Pare, 1805-1873

40. William Pare

Pare was 'small, anomic and bony-faced ... with a large forehead', and a 'tendency to wear threadbare clothes'.[27] Moss described him as dull, despite his somewhat violent speeches.[28] The son of a Birmingham cabinet maker, he was educated at the local grammar school and attended night school at the Birmingham Mechanics Institute. His working life started as an apprentice to his father before becoming a journalist, being variously contributor, editor and printer of the *NMW*. Pare was also successful commercially as a tobacconist, hence his nickname 'Snuffy', and undertook several civic roles, such as a Poor Law Guardian, winning a seat on the first Town Council and becoming a

---

25 Woodward, *Age of Reform*, p.326.
26 Kesteven, pp.38-39.
27 Flick, *BPU*, p.26.
28 Moss, *Attwood*, pp.156, 158.

churchwarden in 1838.[29] He had a foot in many camps, supporting Catholic emancipation and the abolition of church rates. Having previously agreed with Attwood that the then currency system was deficient, he thought the answer lay in co-operative communities. Following several visits to Ralahine, Pare developed Irish connections. Like Owen, he was particularly taken with Thompson's *Inquiry into the Principles of distribution of Wealth most conducive to Human Happiness.* This led to his own book, *Co-operative Agriculture,* though it was not published until 1870. Both Pare and Thompson were more inclined towards setting up small communities, unlike Owen's very large scale ones.

His interest in politics developed whilst attending Attwood's early Newhall Hill meetings from the age of fourteen. As founder of the Birmingham Co-operative Society, he also edited the *Birmingham Co-operative Herald*. He convened the second Congress in Birmingham and was Honorary Secretary to the third Congress in London. He endeavoured to assist with the Derby Lockout and chaired a meeting in Birmingham to raise funds for the victims of the Welsh uprising at Newport in 1839. Sharing Edmondson's interest in statistics, he became a Fellow of the Royal Statistical Society and was the first Superintendent Registrar of Births, Marriages and Deaths for Birmingham. However his dual role caused so much concern that it was debated in the House of Lords.[30] He tried unsuccessfully to hide his involvement with the Rationalists by using initials, but was forced to resign in 1840 and finally left in 1842.

With Attwood's campaigns drawing to an end, and Queenwood in dire straights, Pare relocated to Tytherley. However things had deteriorated even beyond his management skills and he was unable to save it. Pare was one of the few men whose financial assets were not drained by Harmony Hall, though not without a bitter and lengthy legal battle. From the proceeds he was able to purchase the Seville Ironworks in Dublin, which was involved in the building of railway carriages and parts therefor. Owen tried to use Pare as an entrée back into Ireland, but the Lord Lieutenant showed little interest. As a follower of both Owen and Attwood, Garnett described Pare as a link between first-generation Owenites and Co-operation of the second quarter of the nineteenth-century through to its resurgence in the 1870s.[31] He played a prominent part in the London Congress of 1869, when he read a paper on 'co-operative organisation and propaganda'. The meeting was supported *in absentia* by Ruskin, John Stuart Mill, Florence Nightingale and several members of the House of Commons, together with others across Europe.[32]

---
29 Garnett, 'non-Rochdale', p.146.
30 Garnett, *ibid.*, p.147.
31 Garnett, *ibid.*, p.145.
32 Flanagan, Desmond, *Centenary Story of the Co-operative Union* (Manchester 1969), pp.5, 6.

Loyal to Owen right to the end, Pare was one of the mourners at his funeral in Newtown, and became his literary executor in 1858. In his will he left money for an Owen Institute, a Library and a College.[33]

Johann Heinrich Pestalozzi, 1746-1827

The son of a surgeon in Zurich, Pestalozzi was a Swiss social reformer and educator, best known for his promotion of universal education, with focus on the child rather than the teacher in a way which gave freedom for individual development. Not so far removed from Owen, and indeed Government views, but one step ahead, he believed that education would lead people to become responsible citizens and society more peaceful. As Davis and O'Hagan point out, Pestalozzi founded his beliefs on the writings of Rousseau and the importance of learning in infancy and early childhood, thus shattering the myth that Owen was the first to develop infant schools.[34] Pestalozzi also shared Owen's concern for the poor, for whom education was not available at that time. Further, he believed that teaching should become a recognised profession. Pestalozzi establishments continue to flourish, not only in Switzerland, but also in England and many parts of the world.

41. Johann Pestalozzi

George Rapp, 1757-1847

Based mainly on Swedenborg principles, the German-born peasant farmer George Rapp objected to formalised religion. Rapp called himself 'a prophet' and gathered round him a group of followers who sought spiritual instruction. In 1803, following disagreements with the German authorities and separation from the Lutherans, they re-located to Pittsburg in America, the 'land of freedom'. Here he formed a working community, by now 600 in number, which flourished under his leadership. Deciding that Indiana was more suitable, he purchased thirty thousand acres of fertile land and numbers increased to 800. Apart from crops and fruit in abundance, his working community comprised mills, workshops, a tannery, a vineyard and a distillery.[35] It also had two churches, the largest of which Owen used as a meeting hall. However, less popular, were Rapp's ideas on celibacy. He too was called a tyrant by some of his members, who considered themselves to have become his slaves, with past members complaining that they had not been sufficiently rewarded financially. There was also disillusionment when the predicted 'New Coming' did not occur. In order to maintain interest, Rapp

---

33 Garnett, *ibid.,* p.149.
34 Davis and O'Hagan, *Robert Owen,* p.52.
35 Podmore, *biography,* p.286.

decreed that the site was 'unhealthy', and decided to move back to Pittsburg. His Harmony Society survived for a hundred years.

James Rigby, 1806-1862

Rigby worked in a Manchester cotton mill and then became a teacher. He first appears in Co-operative records as having been a delegate from Manchester at the Huddersfield Congress in 1833.[36] Holyoake described Rigby as a popular speaker and an eternal optimist that Owen's new moral world would become a reality.[37] He was 'always endeavouring to do useful work to improve the people', and 'never tasted animal food'.[38] He was a close companion to Owen, being present at his death, and then a prominent member of his Memorial Committee.

Edward Welch, 1806-1868

The Welsh-born Edward Welch may well have been inspired to study architecture when his future employer John Oates from Halifax designed two Church Commissioner churches close to the Welch family home in Wales. Welch moved to Halifax where he trained under Oates. It was here that he met Hansom, and at Welch's instigation they left to form an independent partnership. Working briefly in Yorkshire, they then undertook the church of St John at Toxteth on the outskirts of Liverpool (bombed during the war). Before this was completed, they took on further work on the Isle of Anglesey, during which time they built a goal, the magnificent Victoria Terrace and the Bulkeley Arms in Beaumaris. It was during this period that they jointly undertook the building of Birmingham Town Hall, using stone which was transported from the Penmon quarry on Anglesey. The Birmingham connection and that with the banker Thomas Attwood, who was campaigning for parliamentary reform and universal suffrage, brought them into contact with Robert Owen, building strikes, trade unions and the creation of a Builders' Guildhall. There was no money for the Guildhall and the bankruptcy which the Town Hall brought, along with Welch's marriage to Theodosia Merry of Edgbaston, saw the end of his partnership. He continued to practise independently in Wales and in Yorkshire, and built an hotel and assembly rooms in Birkenhead. However, his practice gradually dwindled and his final employment appears to have been concerned with heating and ventilation installation.

---

36 Brown, *Pathfinders*, p.13.
37 Royle, *millennium*, p.135.
38 Brown, *Pathfinders*, p.13.

SELECT BIBLIOGRAPHY

Primary Sources
Anglesey Archives, Assignment of monies borrowed in connection with the building of Birmingham Town Hall, 23 August 1833, WM/322/3
Birmingham Archives and Collections, Minutes of Street Commissioners of the Street Commissioners relating to the building of the Birmingham Town Hall, 1834, BRO.422407
Dorset Record Office, bills, tenders and letters to J. Firth re. repairs to buildings on estate, 1865-1868, D/WLC/E 39/4, f.40
Hampshire Record Office, Queenwood Prospectus, 47M66/12/1
Notice, 12 September 1833, R.O. 660

Correspondence
Letter Robert Owen to William Allen, 21 April 1825
Letter Pare to *Weekly Free Press,* 11 August 1830
Letter Hansom to Owen, 18 August 1833, R.O. 651
Letter Welch to Owen, 6 September 1833, R.O. 657
Letter Welch to Chantrel esqre., 12 September 1833, R.O. 662
Letter Hansom to Owen, 12 September 1833, R.O. 656
Letter Hansom to Owen, 23 February 1834, R.O. 676
Letter Aldam to Central Board, 8 June 1839

Newspapers and Journals
Birmingham Argus
Birmingham Journal
Freeman's Journal & Daily Commercial Advertiser
Hampshire Chronicle
Leeds Mercury
Monthly Argus
New Harmony Gazette
New Moral World
North Wales Chronicle
Political Register
Poor Man's Guardian
The Architects Magazine

The Builder
The Crisis
The Movement
The Pioneer
The Salisbury and Winchester Journal
The Times

Published (pre 1950)
Booth, Arthur John, *Robert Owen, the founder of Socialism in England* (London, 1869)
Dent, Robert, *Old and New Birmingham,* a history of the town and its people (Birmingham, 1880)
McCabe, Joseph, *Robert Owen* (London, 1920)
Harvey, Rowland Hill, *Robert Owen: social idealist* (Berkeley and Los Angeles, 1949)
Hewitson, Anthony, *History of Preston* (Preston, 1883)
Jones, Lloyd, *The Life, Times, and Labours of Robert Owen,* vol.1 (London, 1890)
Owen, Robert, (ed. M. Beer), *The Life of Robert Owen by Himself* (London, 1920)
Owen, 'The Social System – constitution, laws, and regulations of a community' (1826)
Podmore, Frank, *Robert Owen, a biography* (New Lanark, 1906; reprinted London, 1923)
Postgate, R.W., *The Builders' History* (London, 1923)
Thompson, William, *Practical Directions for the Speedy and Economical Establishment of Communities, on the Principles of Mutual Co-operation, United Possessions and Equality of Exertions and of the means of Enjoyments* (London, 1830)
Wakefield, C.M., *Life of Thomas Attwood* (London, 1885)
Woodward, E.L., *The Age of Reform* (Oxford, 1938)

Secondary Sources
Ashe, Geoffrey, *The Offbeat radicals: The British tradition as alternative dissent* (London, 2007)
Atkins, D.H., *The Church of Ireland: Ecclesiastical Reform and Revolution, 1800-1885* (Newhaven and London, 1971)
Barnsby, George J., *Birmingham Working People – A History of the Labour Movement in Birmingham 1650-1914* (Wolverhampton, 1989)
Briggs, Asa, *A Social History of England,* 3rd edition (London, 1999)
Briggs, Asa, *Victorian Cities* (London, 1991)
Brock, M., *The Great Reform Act* (1973)

Bronowski, J. and Mazlish, Bruce, *The Western Intellectual Tradition* (London, 1960)

Champ, Judith, *A Different Kind of Monk: William Bernard Ullathorne, 1806-1889* (Leominster, 2006)

Claeys, Gregory, *Selected Works of Robert Owen vol.4 The Life of Robert Owen* (London 1993)

Cole, G.D.H., *Robert Owen* (London, 1925): introduction by Margaret Cole *The Life of Robert Owen* (London, 1965)

Cole, Margaret, *Robert Owen of New Lanark* (London, 1953)

Cunningham, Colin, *Victorian and Edwardian Town Halls* (London, 1981)

Davis, Robert and O'Hagan, Frank, *Robert Owen* (London and New York, 2010)

Donnachie, Ian, *Robert Owen: Owen of New Lanark and New Harmony* (East Lothian, 2000)

Duncan, Floyd, *The Utopian Prince, Robert Owen and the Search for Millennium* (revised edition, 2004)

Flick, Carlos, *The Birmingham Political Union and the Movements for Reform in Britain, 1830-1839* (Hamden and London, 1978)

Foot, M.R.D. (ed.), *The Gladstone Diaries* (Oxford, 1978) vol.1

Garnett, Ronald George, *Co-operation and the Owenite socialist communities in Britain 1825-45* (Manchester, 1972)

Gatrell, V.A.C. (ed.), *A New View of Society and report to the County of Lanark* (London, 1969)

Harris, Penelope, *The Architectural Achievements of Joseph Aloysius Hansom (1803-1882), Designer of the Hansom Cab, Birmingham Town Hall and Churches of the Catholic Revival* (Lewiston, 2010)

Harrison, J.F.C., *Robert Owen and the Owenites in Britain and America* (London, 1969)

Hitchcock, Henry-Russell, *Early Victorian Architecture in Britain* (London, 1973)

Hopkins, Eric, *Birmingham: The First Manufacturing Town in the World 1760-1840* (London, 1989)

Kesteven, G.R., *The Triumph of Reform 1832* (London, 1967)

Leigh, J.S., *Preston Cotton Martyrs: The millworkers who shocked a nation* (Lancaster, 2008)

Mansfield, F.A., *The History of Gravesend in the County of Kent* (Rochester, 1981 reprint)

Moss, David, J., *Thomas Attwood, the Biography of a Radical* (Canada, 1990)

Peers, Anthony, *Birmingham Town Hall, An Architecture History* (Farnham, 2012)

Pike, E. Royston (ed.) *Human Documents of the Industrial Revolution* (London, 1966)

Pollard, Sidney and Salt, John, (eds.) *Robert Owen Prophet of the Poor* (London and Basingstoke, 1971)

Reekes, Andrew, *Speeches that changed Britain: Oratory in Birmingham* (Alcester, 2015)
Royle, Edward, *Robert Owen and the commencement of the millennium* (Manchester, 1998)
Salmon, Frank, *Building on Ruins* (Ashgate, 2000)
Stansky, Peter, *Gladstone: A Progress in Politics* (New York, London, 1979)
Stevenson, Graham, *Defence or Defiance? Derbyshire and the fight for democracy* (Croydon, 2014)
Thompson, Noel & Williams, Chris, (ed.), *Robert Owen and his Legacy* (Cardiff, 2011)

Contributions

Peter Brock, 'The Socialists of the Polish Great Emigration', in Asa Briggs and John Saville (eds.) *Essays in Labour History* (London, 1967)
Butt, John, 'Robert Owen and Trade Unionism', in Four Essays: *Robert Owen, Industrialist, Reformer, Visionary 1771-1858* (London, 1971)
Gilley, Sheridan, 'Industrialization, Empire, Identity', in Sheridan Gilley and W.J. Sheils (eds.), *A History of Religion in Britain: practice and belief from pre-Roman times to the present* (Oxford, 1994)
Harrison, John, 'Robert Owen and the Communities', in Four Essays: *Robert Owen, Industrialist, Reformer, Visionary 1771-1858* (London, 1971)
Himmelfarb, Gertrude, 'The Culture of Poverty' in H.J. Dyos and Michael Wolff (eds.), *The Victorian City: A Body of Troubles*, vol.VI (London, 1973)
McDowell, R.B., 'The Protestant Nation 1775-1800' in Moody, T.W. and Martin, F.X. (eds.), *The Course of Irish History* (New York, 1967).
Woolf, Michael and Fox, Celina, 'Pictures from the Magazines' in H.J. Dyos and Michael Wolff (eds.), *The Victorian City: Ideas in the Air*, vol.V (London, 1973)

Directories

Gillow, Joseph, *A Literary and Biographical History or Bibliographical Dictionary of the English Catholics from the Breach with Rome in 1534 to the Present Time* (London, 1885)
Oxford Dictionary of National Biographies (online version)
A History of the County of Warwickshire, Victoria County History, Warwick, vol.7, City of Birmingham

Articles

Briggs, Asa, 'Thomas Attwood and the economic background of the Birmingham Political Union', *Cambridge Historical Journal*, 9 (1947-9)
Briggs, Asa, 'Co-operation: from Community Building to Shopkeeping' in early nineteenth-century England, in Asa Brigs, *Essays in Labour Industry* (London, 1967)

Brooks, Michael, 'The Builder' in the 1840s: The Making of a Magazine, the Shaping of a Profession', *Victorian Periodicals Review*, 14, no.3 (Fall, 1981)

Burgess, Charles, 'The Boatload of Trouble: William Maclure and Robert Owen Revisited', *Indiana Magazine of History,* XCIV, (June 1998)

Garnett, R.G., 'William Parr, A non-Rochdale Pioneer', *Co-operative Review* (May, 1964)

Holyoake, George J., 'A Visit to Harmony Hall', published in *The Movement* (November, 1844)

O'Connor, Dennis, 'Thomas McDonnell: A 19th Century Pastor of St Peter's Gloucester', *Gloucestershire Catholic History Society Journal,* 32, 1997

Oliver, W.H., 'The labour exchange phase of the co-operative movement', *Oxford Economic Paper,* October 1958

Personal Life of George Grote in 'Thomas Attwood and the economic background of the Birmingham Political Union', *Cambridge Historical Journal* vol.1x, no.2 (London, 1948)

Pitzer, Donald E., 'The Original Boatload of Knowledge Down the Ohio River: William Maclure's and Robert Owen's Transfer of Science and Education to the Midwest, 1825-26', *Ohio J. Sci.* 89 (5): 128-142, 1989

Salmon, Frank, 'Storming the Campo Vaccino': British Architects and the Antique Buildings of Rome after Waterloo, *Architectural History*, 38 (1995)

Theses

Allen, Clare Bridget, 'Joseph Hansom Architect 1803-1882' (unpublished BA, Manchester University, 1977)

Champ, Judith, F., 'Assimilation and Separation: the Catholic Revival in Birmingham c1640-1850', (unpublished doctoral thesis, University of Birmingham, 1984)

Evinson, Denis, 'Joseph Hansom' (unpublished Masters dissertation, University of London, 1966)

Other

Barnsby, George, J., *Robert Owen and the First Socialists in the Black Country* (extract from *The Working Class Movement in the Black Country 1750-1867,* u.d.)

Hansom, Joseph, 'A Statement of Facts relative to the Birmingham Town-Hall, and an Appeal to the Rate-Payers and Inhabitants of Birmingham' (Birmingham, 1834)

Morton, *Life and ideas ...* (London, 1962): general account of life and work of Robert Owen by means of extracts from his own writings *Robert Owen, Industrialist, Reformer, Visionary, 1771-1858:* four essays (Margaret Cole *et al*) (London, 1971) – written to mark second centenary of his birth

www.jhpestalozzi.org

INDEX

(*Illustrations marked in* **bold**)

Acts of Parliament:
  Great Reform Bill, 45, 47, 55, 73, 76, 135, 136
  Metropolitan Building Act, 58
  Municipal Corporations, 44, 74
  Poor Law Amendment Act, 26, 57
Aldam, Heaton, 96, 100
Allen, William, 28, 29-30, 31, 103, 116, 117, 134-135, **134**
Anglesey, 44, 45, 49, 50, 54, 82, 145
Association of All Classes of All Nations, 86, 94
Attwood, Thomas, 45, 46, 47, 48, 55, **63**, 73, 75-77, 83, 84, 86, **88**, 135-136, **135**, 142, 143

Barry, Sir Charles, 52, 59, 121
Beaumaris (Bulkeley Arms, gaol, Trainer's house, Victoria Terrace), 45n, **62**, 145
Bentham, Jeremy, 29, 135
Birmingham, 44, 45, 47, 48, 50, 52, 53, 55, 60, **65**, **87**, **89**, 94, 121, 135, 136, 139, 141
  Builders' Union, 51, **66**, 84, 94
  Co-operative Society, 73, 77, 78, 121
  Equitable Labour Exchange, 83-84, **91**, 95
  Free Grammar School, 51-53
  Labour Notes, 52, 80, 82-83
  Operative Builders' Guildhall, 53-54, **67**, 99, 145
  Saint Monday, 72
  Street Commissioners, 45, 46-47, 49, 51, 60, 74-75, 82

Town Hall, **front cover**, 44, 45, 46-50, **46**, 53, 60, 64, **64**, 73
Boulton, Matthew, 72
Bromsgrove Lickey Memorial, 82, **90**
Brougham, Henry, Lord, 18, 116, 118, 137
Bulkeley, Sir Richard, 49

Cobbett, William, 28, 34, 121, 136
Co-operative Congresses, 77, 80, 93, 94, 96, 97, 102, 121, 143, 145
Communities:
  Harmony Hall **front cover**, 33, 70, 73, 84, **112**, **113**, **115**, 117, 123, 138, 139, 140, 143
  Motherwell, 92
  Orbiston, 92
  New Harmony, 93, 98, 107, 117, 119, 123, 138
  New Lanark, 18, 30, 31, 32, 33, 34, **38**, **39**, **40**, 51, 70, 72, 77, 81, 82, 83, 93, 103, 104, 106, 116, 117, 123, 135, 137, 140
  Ralahine, 73, 77, 79, 82, 93, 95, 117, 143
  Spa Fields, 92

Derby, 46
  Lockout, 48, **68**, 85
Doherty, James, 84, 85, 121

East Tytherley, see also Harmony Hall, 93, 94, 95, 96, **111**, **115**

Edge, Charles, 74, 75n
Edmondson, George, 105-109, 123, 137-138, 143
education, 18, 20, 22, 23, 24, 25, 27, 28, 29, 33, 34, 35, 51, 54, 59, 60, 72, 106, 107, 120, 123, 137, 138, 140, 144
Exeter, Bishop of, 95

factory reform, 22, 28, 123
Fellenberg, Philipp Emanuel von, 27
Fielden, John, 121
Finch, John, 95, 96, 98, 102, 104
Foster, John, 45
French Revolution, 79, 140, 142
Fretageot, Mme. Marie, 32, 117, 138, 140

Galpin, William, 98, 139
Gibson, John, 118, 121, 122
Goldsmid, Isaac Lyon, 92, 96
Grand National Consolidated Trades Union (GNCTU), 55, 56, 80, 83, 84-85, 123
Green, Charles Federick, 98, 105

Hansom, Henry John, 120
Hansom, Joseph Aloysius **front cover**, 73, 75, 76, 77, 80, 82, 84, 85, 94, 99, 100, 101, 105, 108, 122, 123, 124, **125**
  family background, 43-44, 120-121
  hansom cab, 119, 122, 124, **130**
  The Builder, 57-59, **69**, 97, 102, 119, 124, 136
Hansom, Joseph Stanislaus, 43, 121, 122

151

Hansom, Charles, 121, 134, 141
Harmony Hall, see
  Communities and
  Queenwood
Hinckley, 55, 56, 57
Holyoake, George Jacob, 33, 96, 101, 102, 118, **139**

Ireland, 46, 73, 76, 77, 78, 79-80, 84, 93, 137, 143

Kent, Duke of, 20, 29, 117
Knowledge, Boatload of, 32

Leeds, St Mary's church, 120, **126**
Loudon, John Claudius, 58, 101

Maclure, William, 29, 30, 32, 33, 35, 116, 117, 138, 140, **140**
Manchester, 19-20, 50, 52, 53, 71, 72, 75, 84, 85, 93, 94, 121, 136, 137, 139
  Literary and Philosophical Society, 116
Macdonald, Captain Donald, 31, 34
McDonnell, Thomas, 76, 78-79, 95, 140-141, **140**, 142
Mechanics Institute, 77, 106, 142
music, 25, 30, 48, 75, 103, 104, 108

Neef, Josef, 32, 34, 117, 119, 140
New Harmony (see communities)
New Lanark (see communities)
Newtown, Powys, 17, 18, **36**, 118, 124, 144

Oates, John, 44, 145
O'Connell, Daniel, 73, 75, 76, 77, 79-80, 136, 141, 142, **142**
Oestreicher, Albert, 103, 104
Owen, Robert, **front cover**, 37, 45, 46, 48, 50, 51, 53, 54, 56, 57, 70, 71, 72, 73, 76, 79, 80, 81, 82, 83, 84, 85, 86, 92, 93, 94, 96, 97, 99, 100, 101, 102, 103, 104, 122, 123, **125**, 135, 138, 143, 144
  family background, 17-18, 19
  Four Essays, 21-22, 25
  Owen's Plan, 25, 26, 28, 29, **41**, 93, 94, 138
  religion, 19, 25, 29, 30, 35, 94, 118, 122, 123, 135, 139, 140, 144
  Report to the County of Lanark, 25, 28, 93, 96
  New Moral World, 22, 25, 86, 97, 98, 101, 104
  The Crisis, 25, **42**, 56, 83, 85
  The Pioneer, 25, 55, 56, 84, 85
Owen, Robert Dale, 22, 27, 31, 32, 34, 117, 118, 119
Owen, David, 117, 119
Owen, William, 27, 31, 32, 33, 119

Pare, William, 55, 73, 75, 76, 77-78, 79, 81, 82, 86, 93, 94, 95, 99, 118, 138, 142-44, **142**
Pestalozzi, Johann, 27, 32, 34, 104, 117, 119, 138, 140, 144, **144**
Peterloo, battle of, 48n, 55
Phillips, Matthew, 44
Political Unions, 46, 48, 55, 73, 75, 80, 81-82, 136
Preston, 105
  cotton martyrs, 23n
  St Walburge's Church, 119, **127**
  schools, 59

Queenwood, 105, 106, 107, 108, 109, 117, 118, 123, 134, 138, 143

Rapp, George, 31, 34, 93, 102, 144
Rational Religionists, Universal Community Society of, 86, **91**, 94, 95, 103, 105, **110**, 140

Reid, Richard James, 105
Rigby, James, 94, 99, 103, 116, 118, 145

Science, Halls of, 105, 118
slave trade, 23, 134
Spooner, Isaac, 45-46, **63**, 137n
St Beuno's College, St Asaph, 120, **128**
Stamford, Lincolnshire, 19

The Builder (see Hansom)
The Crisis (see Owen)
The New Moral World (see Owen)
The Pioneer (see Owen)
Todmorden Hall, 121, **129**
Toldpuddle Martyrs, 85
trade unions, 54, 80, 94, 145
Triennial Music Festivals, 46, 47, 141
Tulketh Hall, 105, 106, 107, **114**, 137, 138
Tyndall, John, 108, 109, p.134n.

Ullathorne, Bishop William, 121

Vandeleur, John Scott, 79, 93, 95

Walthew, Matthew, 52, 53
Welch, Edward, 44, 49, 50, 51, 52, 53, 54, 55, 73, 84, 145
Welch, John, 82
Wellington, Duke of, 55, 73, 136
Wilberforce, William, 22, 134, 137n
Whitwell, Thomas Stedman, 32, 34
working hours, 21, 22, 23, 72, 81, 82, 85, 103, 121, 123, 137

York, 43, 44, **61**